Our hearts hang from the lemon trees

Our hearts hang from the lemon trees

Laetitia Rutherford

CB

Copyright © Laetitia Rutherford 2013

Laetitia Rutherford has asserted her right under the Copyright,
Designs and Patents Act 1988 to be identified as the
author of this work. All rights reserved. No part of this publication
may be reproduced, stored in a retrieval system or transmitted in any
form, or by any means (electronic, mechanical, or otherwise) without
the prior written permission of both the copyright owners
and the publisher.

A CIP catalogue record for this book
is available from the British Library.

ISBN 978-1-78072-172-9

Printed and bound by CPI Group (UK) Ltd, Croydon, CR0 4YY

Cover design: Andrew Smith

CONTENTS

PREFACE

All childhoods come to an end, and all families do too. My family was a divided one, divided by the strangeness of its characters and by endings that came too soon. I started out writing one story, but here I have written another. It is a confession about my family and about myself. It is about how I found solace in the book within this book, and how I came to terms with my memories of what was lost. On this journey, I found both instructions on to how to live and, by an arcane route, I recovered a simple secret of happiness.

FRANCE

The house was set a few hundred paces back from the sea, up a shallow incline that turned into a private road. Two enormously high palm trees flanked the gate, with its large black iron bell operated by a chain that would have made a fierce noise if anybody ever pulled it. We arrived after a three-day journey, Mum and us three girls. As the car slowed down, the wheels emitted a delicious crunch over gravel. My grandmother came out to greet us in her summer casuals, button-down striped cotton dress, bare legs in white loafers and pearls exchanged for coloured beads, with her butler-of-sorts Patmanathan following behind. She wore her theatrical smile, slightly manic, a glint in the eye but with a hardness too, and gave us all a brief bear hug as we chanted greetings. After that, it was swiftly into the routine: tea at five o'clock, then baths before putting on dresses for dinner. My grandfather sat in a favourite armchair and stroked our heads one by one, repeating, '*Elles ont bonne mine.*' Our youth and health verified in this way, he kept quiet. His took his role on the fringes of my grandmother's management of the household.

When I was old enough to move from the cot at my grandmother's bedside, I slept with my sisters and cousins in the blue room and the pink room upstairs, across the landing, through a sliding door and down a few steps into a little apartment. Often I lay wide awake on the bed underneath the big shutters flung open to the night, watching the rhythmic beam of the lighthouse, listening to the crickets chirrup and every hour the bong of the grandfather clock at the foot of the staircase. Ever since then, the beam of a lighthouse, or the warble of doves just beyond the window at dawn, or the smell of heat off the tarmac in the afternoon, has reminded me of that lighthouse, those doves in the morning, that heat. I listened to that house breathe and creak through twenty long summers, often bored, or longing to be somewhere else, always ensnared by its charm.

As part of my grandmother's rambunctious efforts to make us into joiners equipped for the outdoors, she personally gave us new haircuts and bought us new swim-wear at the beginning of the holidays. The haircut took place in the middle of the hall, clumps of fair hair disap-pearing with a few snatches of the kitchen scissors, lost against the green marble of the floor and quickly swept away from its cool hard surface. Sometimes this ritual was interrupted by the loud trilling of the telephone, the ear and mouthpiece of its cream-coloured receiver as round and shiny as my grandmother's coiffure. She answered the phone with an accusatory '*Allo?*' and then, for reasons known only to herself, using a pseudonym: *'Oui, içi Madame Robert.'* The matter dealt with, she turned to us and declared that we were now decked out with a 'snazzy Antibes haircut', and took out the new garments from her Monoprix bag: trunks... boys' trunks. They came in two colours, navy blue and turquoise. Naturally I opted for the turquoise ones, as they were that bit girlier than the navy ones.

Every day revolved around getting to the beach, to the sea — where everything is forgiven and renewed, and which still seems to me the point and destination of any journey. My mother had spent some of her childhood summers on those same beaches, and no summer went by when she didn't remind us that in her day the Garoupe, the main beach made famous by Picasso and the roaring 1920s sets, was nothing but rocks and sand all the way to the point. We walked and clambered that distance along the point over and over again, a wind and sun-beaten coastline where cactus grows close to pine and cedar and where high walls now hide the houses of the very rich. Antibes is an ancient town, a western window on the world beyond Europe. It was first used as a port by the Ancient Greeks, who called it Antipolis. After them came the Romans, who built the fortifications of the old town, which are still largely intact. Ramparts run along the steep verge between land and sea, forming a promenade for holidaymakers and looking over a bay known as the Bay of Angels.

On Sunday mornings, we went to mass in the cathedral, which was crammed into a small square between pink-walled buildings spilling geraniums from grey shuttered windows. Inside, we sat in half-darkness, listening to the Latin mass performed by an ancient priest almost completely obscured by his vestments and the incense from his swinging censer. As we emerged into the hot sun afterwards, dazed by the contrast and the clang of bells, the old men drinking on the steps to the entrance stretched out their mottled hands to beg. Through the stone archway we headed, in a few paces stumbling directly into the wide market square, half enclosed by canvas and teeming with fruit sellers, pungent cheeses and chickens on spits. On its other side the ramparts soared, and at last there was the massive sky and clean sea air. Nestled against the sea wall, rising sheer out of the rocks overlooking the sea, was a medieval remnant, the Château Grimaldi, which became the first ever Picasso museum and is still the loveliest.

These were all-female parties to church and to the market, crossing the three generations. But occasionally my grandfather took us girls out in his big old slate-grey BMW. Down in the Midi, he wore his holiday uniform of a blue Lacoste polo shirt and a *casquette* made of basket weave. Hats were kept in the black bathroom, on hooks laden with an assortment of canvas, straw, gabardine, rumpled cotton and rattan. Hats on, we'd scramble onto the grey corduroy back seat. The only sign of colour in the have been united mostly in our incapacity, but they didn't know what stories we made up about our errant relatives. As a young man, my grandfather had been a brilliant rider, people said. He could make a horse curtsy or step sideways, and do tricks like balancing a broom on the end of his nose. If he hadn't become a diplomat, he always said he would have been a jockey. He had the compact physique and the instinctive approach, but I found it hard to imagine that speed and wiry energy at work. Occasionally we wandered through the house to look at his wine. In the black bathroom, a child-size wrought-iron gate opened to a set of stone steps. It was much colder in the bathroom, made completely of stone and black ceramic, any light from the deep-set window reflected only from a set of bronze fish-shaped taps. Down the steps we went to the *cave*, I swallowing my fear of what could be down there, deprived of sun and air. We sat on crates lit by a lantern. A smell of damp stone settled on my skin, and my grandfather started to run his fingers along the racks and pick up bottles. His hands seemed cork-like to me, patched with darker stains and faintly lined. Objects made an imprint on them and flattened the tips of his fingers, and it took a while for these impressions to leave his skin. First things first: '*Il y a les rouges,*' he said, sweeping a layer of dust from a bottle and pausing with a laboured breath as if accosted by the face of an old friend, '*et il y a les blancs.*' We moved on to the Bordeaux and the Bourgognes, but never much further than that.

It was rare to see my grandfather in the kitchen. I assumed he didn't know how to do anything in there, but we wandered in and without fuss he demonstrated how to make vinaigrette. He did it wordlessly, as if to show the inarguability of this skill, how it was integral to a decent way of life, and how I had this chance to memorise it from him. Lunch and dinner were not complete without a bowl of salad — a glass, silver or wooden bowl of pure green leaves tossed with walnut wood spoons. The smooth tartness of vinaigrette is one of the deeply refreshing sensations that will always be tied to that stretch of Mediterranean coast for me, like the astringent cool of salt water penetrating the roots of my hair. The best way to make vinaigrette is my grandfather's simple method: measuring it by sight straight into the bottom of the bowl. First a spoonful of mustard for spice, and a spoonful of mayonnaise, as that is what makes the oil and vinegar emulsify, then he poured in the cloudy green oil and translucent red vinegar with a steady hand in a practised balance, the vinegar neither thinning nor making the whole too sharp, the oil not turning it too unctuous and flat. Finally he added a pinch of sugar to help the flavours combine, and occasionally another pinch — this time of dried dill — to round out the kick of a good vinaigrette. The salad leaves were suspended just above the mixture in the bowl so they lost none of their form and could be tossed just before eating.

Most of the time, my grandfather and I sat together

in his library, making up stories in our own franglais, a mixture of French, English and baby talk. He had a collection of toy soldiers from when he was a boy, each one painted the vivid red of the French army in the days before camouflage, and a lead weight in the palm of my hand. Picking up a book with the same casual curiosity with which he picked up one of these toys, he counselled me never to read one all the way through, but to skim the beginning, then go straight on to the end, the sort of approach that would have appalled my father. As my grandfather was a wide reader, and spent much of his time writing his memoirs, this advice was oddly disingenuous. It was a kind of dare not to take an idea too seriously, not to get carried away by one point of view and not to waste too much time thinking. This mixture of nonchalance and pragmatism was easy when you had already read so much and seen so much of the world. It was neither 'do what I say', nor 'do what I do', but 'see if you can be what I am', a dare made with all the knowledge of it not being possible. But it was my grandmother who made it clear that none of the younger generation could live up to them.

My grandfather knew even the most obscure verses of the nursery rhymes we had sung in the car with my mother all the way from London. *Le bon roi Dagobert avait sa culotte à l'envers* was the funniest, sung in his slow and congested baritone, about the old king who put his pants on inside out, got chased off the hunt by a rabbit and ate too much cake. But the one that never failed to charm was about the little sailor who went out on the *Mer Mé-Mé-di terranée ohé ohé*. When the crew ran out of food, they did a straw poll to find out who would be eaten, and the little sailor pulled the short straw. He put up a prayer and all of a sudden the sea filled with fish, saving the boy's life. My uncles' old comic books, *Asterix* and *Tintin*, were on the shelves in Paris, but in the South were the more old-fashioned books like *Les Fables de La Fontaine* and the Gallimard anthologies, easily spotted from their identical white covers with the black lettering and ribbons spun into their gold-tooled spines. Despite the insouciance he claimed, my grandfather knew the words from these anthologies without ever having to open them. He liked the rhyming ones and the sentimental ones, perhaps because he knew their appeal to children. There was one I always remembered because in it was a message about how to live and the things that mattered. It was just the sort of thing my grandfather came up with, and had his way of making the subtle seem effortless. The little poem described what was right in front of me, an idea of home and happiness, but a scene that also seemed just outside my reach.

Je souhaite dans ma maison
Une femme ayant sa raison
Un chat passant parmi les livres
Des amis en toute saison
Sans lesquels je ne peux pas vivre

Stroking my hair, my grandfather would challenge me to do a more convincing purr than he could. Our cat was called Chloé, and had a very loud purr. But like all cats, she was never around when you wanted her. Sometimes, playing in the garden, I could hear my grandfather calling from his chair inside, a short, sharp '*Chloé? Chloé?*' He would be lucky if she turned up, and he increasingly lacked the energy to get up and find her. She was a Siberian — longhaired and grey, more wild-looking than elegant — that he had found asleep under a pile of snow on the bonnet of his car one winter. Our stories would get more elaborate as the grandfather clock bonged another hour away, and there was still no sign of the others. The last chapter had us locking them all in the *cave* while we raided the shopping, but this was always cut short by the sound of car wheels on the gravel.

In the evenings we had dinner on the terrace on a large table that stayed outside, partly because it was imperishable and partly because it was almost too heavy to move. It took two men to part shepherd, part roll the marble top along its circumference, with my grandmother a frantic umpire, shouting for it not to smash her china or crack itself. Its wrought-iron base screeched horribly against the stone flags if you pushed it hard enough. The ceiling of this terrace was made of moulded plaster painted in pale green, a model of grass transposed to the ceiling in a lush landscape that had no grass. I spent much of every dinner watching lizards dart across it, heading for the corners, their skins sometimes bright, sometimes obscure against the background.

My grandfather allowed water to be mixed with wine for those who wanted something lighter to drink, particularly my mother, who was considered to have barely graduated into the same league of adulthood as them. The glass refracted the last rays of sun, making it shine through the watered wine with the colour of the evening. He also mixed different wines together, smiling ambiguously when guests praised the wine he had sloshed together from his collection. As it was always served in decanters, nobody ever knew where it came from anyway.

After the artichokes, either warm with melted salted butter, or cold with vinaigrette, we waited for the sign for the next step from my grandmother. We dipped our fingers in the water in the little glass bowls next to our places, floating with the petals I had collected from the garden before dinner. I watched my grandmother constantly turning and turning the dessert spoon and fork that lay above her plate, between her wine and water glasses and her napkin ring, betraying her nerves in spite of the graceful ideal she insisted on. She was describing a friend of hers, a 'Mimi de la something', saying that she was '*charmante, mais charmante, mais tellement raffinée*'. As she elaborated on her theme of this woman's distinction, the delicacy of her own powers of judgment in seeing this, and the implied intimacy of their friendship therefore, she left her fiddling to wave a hand before her. Coiling her hand through the air, teasing the delicate weave of her friend's brilliance this way, she carried on talking about her beautiful house, her wonderful dinners, her fabulous jewellery. Few came in for such praise; only her other friend, Madame la Duchesse, came in for more. But it didn't stop the inevitable judgment being slipped in, as to whether the person had 'pots of money' and beautiful things '*en pagaille*', or 'not a bean'. Then she tapped her knife on the side of her glass — her signal for the plates to be taken away.

My older sister, Emma, always sat closest to my grandmother and it was clear that she was the favourite. The impenetrable logic of 'before you were born' must have held sway here; they must have established a hidden contract back then that gave them a special relationship. Perhaps it was because she was very blonde and fair-skinned and needed extra care as a result, beside the unchangeable virtue of being the oldest. She was not subjected to the boys' trunks, but had a bikini with bow ties. Emma had been to the house over Easter, when the garden was a different place. The orange tree at the back of the house produced a small fruit at that time, emerging in a miracle of birth from a cold that nearly killed it each year. Roses flourished then in the year's first sun, fat velvet cabbages too thirsty to survive as the summer drew near. I pictured this mostly from hearsay, as my middle sister, Milla, and I stayed at the house only once at Easter, when Emma needed peace and quiet to do her Common Entrance. But she had spent Easters there over her birthday, when the windows at the end of the *salon* were crowded with the yellow pom-pom blooms of the mimosa tree. 'Remember your cake, lambkin,' my grandmother was saying to her still as we ate our dinner, 'decorated with mimosa flowers?' The image of this cake, and a tea party under the tree lit with the yellow of spring, lodged in my mind. It was an amazing cake, deserving of its genus name angel, as inside it was the palest buttery crumb and over the top floated hundreds of perfectly spherical yellow flowers.

In the daytime, Patmanathan wore a shirt, jeans and espadrilles and did anything from unblocking the kitchen sink to repainting the garage door. The house rang with the shrill operatic cry of my grandmother calling 'Patmanathan! Patmanathan!' It was like the call of a lost religion, an involuntary statement of need, though it always carried the hint of my grandmother's conviction that Patmanathan fell a step short of her instructions. At dusk, he changed into a white high-buttoned jacket and white gloves in order to serve dinner. He was closer in age to us than my mother, supporting a young wife far away in war-torn Sri Lanka and children who were younger than us, which meant somehow that we were on the same side. We knew about his young family from hanging around the kitchen counters with him when my grandmother was elsewhere, but most of the time she commanded the situation, which required his silence and absolute assent. The question of his papers sometimes arose, though I never knew whether my grandmother ultimately helped him in giving him a job and a place to sleep, or if she was exploiting the vulnerability of his lack of citizenship – likely an unspoken balance between the two that ensured the interdependence between him and her. A sly glance from the corner of her eye as he served dinner was a mark of her approval that she had oiled the machine correctly, and she was relaxed enough to gossip freely.

Many guests came once, only to be excluded from my grandmother's table for a punishing few years. She had made a career of giving parties, for almost fifty years playing host to my grandfather's receptions in French headquarters in the world's political hotspots and France's former colonies. But in a lifetime of making friends and connections, she had also made enemies, undermining other diplomats' wives for their ugly clothes, their unacceptable accents, their inedible menus. Her highest form of praise was for a wife who had 'beautiful taste' and who was '*tout à fait correcte*', her house 'absolutely tickety-boo'. The worst crime was having 'absolutely no taste' and generally exhibiting 'the manners of a guttersnipe', by blowing their noses with two hands or using dread expressions like 'I'm pleased to meet you'.

She mingled the English phrases with the French and

American ones she acquired through marriage. Both my grandparents had started out somewhere completely different, my grandmother from a Gloucestershire family of stockbrokers, and my grandfather from a rich merchant family near Lyon. They took the strange decision in the eyes of both families – firstly to marry from opposite sides of the Channel, and then to leave France with the Foreign Ministry. They spent most of their long marriage travelling and living in the best houses a city could offer, with the best cars and the best domestic help. Returning to France in retirement, when we, the grandchildren, came along, their roots looked different and shallower. In her house and at her table, my grandmother operated a severe policy of who was in and who was out, with a fervour that I imagined grew from ruling the roost in foreign embassies and indulging in all the exemptions and official welcomes a diplomatic life brings with it. My grandmother still tried to use the defunct 'D' for diplomatic on the back of her car; rather than throw the battered sign away, she kept it on view in the boot of her Renault.

Their youngest son fell victim to one of her excommunications due to one insolent act that leaked its after-effects in the house for years. It revealed what seemed to my hushed and baffled understanding a fatal weakness in my uncle's character, but possibly an even greater one in his relationship with his mother. One year, after the summer holidays and in the wake of my grandfather's retirement from the Foreign Ministry, he sent his parents a thank-you letter addressing his father by his name alone, dropping the title 'Monsieur l'Ambassadeur'. This son had always seemed a questionable figure to them for his rebelliousness – he had worn his hair long as a teenager and wanted to write songs and play the guitar in a band. He had never been the favourite. That was their second son, with his film star looks and glamorous girlfriends. But he was also the only one of their sons, and the only child other than my mother, who had married and produced grandchildren. His two daughters, close in age to us, were our only cousins and my mother and her brother shared the urge to offer us up for the adoration of grandparents, and perhaps at the same time receive from them love and congratulations. Yet the hierarchy of favouritism they had suffered as children continued to exist, diverting onto us in weaker form.

The absence of my uncle and his family after this dereliction of respect was the elephant in the house for five summers. He was finally admitted back again, but after this long absence, the threat of possible future expulsion hovered in the air. Then there was the guest who touched the side of the coffee pot, asking, 'Is it hot?' The story of this affront was repeated again and again: '"Is it hot?" she asked me, in my house! My godfathers. Touching the silver! Even if it were stone cold, how could you be so rude? As if my house were a hotel, a hotel that doesn't work!' Worst of all, according to my grandmother were her husband's family (and their misdeeds were rarely dredged up). My grandfather had a large family living perhaps all over France, but it was as though they had been cut off in a long-past feud nobody talked about any more. My grandmother seemed to have completely forgotten her own family, or what was left of it. Her parents were long dead and her brother had immigrated to Australia where he had become a priest. She seemed affectionate towards him, but their relationship was safely contained in the annual letter received during his winter, our summer, and its report about the weather and the continued health of his wife and daughters.

After our main course came the cheese, always a hard cheese, a soft cheese, a blue cheese and a goat's cheese, before a dessert of sorbet, chocolate mousse, or, if it was just family, simply fruit. We didn't go into the kitchen after dinner, but in the quiet we could hear the cuckoo clock, the voice of kitsch incongruous with the rest of the house. It came ahead of the solemn bong of the grand father clock, as we headed upstairs, pulling the fat silk rope of banister in mock tiredness. English rhymes from my grandmother's childhood shuttled around with us as we darted from room to room, eventually settling in our allocated beds. '*Do you remember an inn, Miranda? Do you remember an inn? And the fleas that tease in the high Pyrenees and the wine that tasted of tar.*' Although she was English, my grandmother's past seemed so far away she may as well have spent her childhood in the mysterious inn with its acrobat insects and character-building wine. I was so relieved to be finally big enough not to be made to sleep in a cot by her bed, as I had done as a toddler, perhaps to give my mother a break from tiny children. I didn't believe my grandmother thought much of the arrangement either; it was one of those accidents where the smallest gets the trappings of babyhood for the longest, handed down in a last hurrah from the older ones. '*Far and few, far and few are the lands where the Jumblies live. Their heads are green and their hands are blue...*' There was much more fun to be had chattering about the Jumblies once I was able to share rooms with my sisters.

Lying in bed at night under the open window, I watched the lighthouse beam its rhythmic arc across the sky and the treetops. I could hear my grandmother and Patmanathan at their nightly ritual in the kitchen below. Everything needed to be cleaned, and if not done properly, cleaned again, not using too much soap or too much water. She kept a jar with a quarter-inch of washing-up liquid by the sink, the full bottle underneath at the back of the cupboard, in case her irresponsible dependants squirted too much over the greasy pots. I occasionally heard his murmurs of assent, 'Yes, madame. Yes, madame,' and knew he was nodding his head from side to side, in the way that left an infuriating doubt in my grandmother's mind as to whether he really meant 'yes'. Left to themselves after the rest of us had gone to bed, all the irritations of the day broiling up to a fever pitch, her voice climbed higher and louder as she laid into his faults and negligence. The smell of frying onions and spices rose up to the window, as he could not eat his own dinner until ours was cleared away, and my grandmother went on, picking and yowling at his failures. If she wasn't ready to go to sleep, then he couldn't be ready either.

❦

In the mornings, the sea was so blue it was almost painful to see its perfection. We longed to get to the beach as quickly as possible, but there was always some hanging around to be done first as my mother and grandmother debated the gardening, or if there were the right supplies for dinner. There was a dry well near the vines on the terrace side of the house, filled in with earth to a depth I could jump into and climb out of. It was springy under my feet, thick with the dried seedlings of pine trees. The pinecones dropped by the trees seemed too shiny and intricate to leave to rot under the bushes, but often, you picked one up and already a section was desiccated. I could hear my grandmother calling 'Lisbet! Lisbet!' Only she used this diminutive for my mother, a high extended note at the end of it. 'Yes, Ma,' my mother answered in the more down-to-earth tone I knew as a response from my own childishly frantic repetitive call to her. I recognised the way she tried to give a definitive answer, with a decisive beat unlike the insistently needy calling of her mother and her children. Whatever they were debating was easily sidetracked by old bugbears.

'We hardly ever went to Les Vallières when we were little,' my mother was saying, referring to the house where my grandfather grew up. 'Don't you remember we went to see Bonpapa and Bonnemaman that time, when little Oliver was born?' my grandmother gave her own version. 'We went to show them your new brother. We had tea in the yellow salon, and they didn't have anything to offer, saying the *pâtissier* had failed to deliver. I remember it so well, inviting us to tea and no cake to serve. And that's when Bonnemaman said to me, '*Nous avons donné Les Ormes à Madeleine.*' My godfathers! When Daddy had left me to look after you when he was in China, or Canada. *Nous avons donné Les Ormes à Madeleine.*'

I could see another pinecone under the bushes at the level of my sightline over the top of the well. It was the name of a house they were talking about and, to the outrage of my grandmother, the house was being given away to one of my grandfather's sisters, rather than to his wife. 'But you'll always have the house in Washington,' my grandmother was saying, alluding again to places elsewhere, properties taken and investments made in another life. Their conversation was scattered with fragments of these off-scene projects, and the complications of 'opening up' and 'shutting down' the house. A whole morning could be devoted to sorting through piles of keys, all of them with tags and incomprehensible labels, some rolled in ancient plastic bags or placed in envelopes with the sticky part yellowed and brittle. Convinced of the absolute urgency of these tasks, my grandmother was all sighs and loud whistles of breath, emitting the American exclamation 'Brother!' followed by '*Ah la la la la la*' over again. We needed to be closely on hand to fetch or fix small things, and in case we missed the signal that the adults were ready to go. Finally we assembled flippers, masks, buckets, straw mats, and made it out of the house.

Down on the beach, we were in and out of the sea all day long. The salt slaked on our skins and the smell of *frites* and *crèpes* cooking on the beach were sensations so rich in themselves yet so sharply delineated. It was impossible not to feel more alive in being able to feel them all at once. For years, we wore nothing but swim things, a t-shirt and flipflops, out on the beach every day with buckets and nets. There were starfish and crabs, but the iconic find of every summer was the octopus, far more dangerous and disgusting. Its tentacles differed strangely in length, and its entire body other than its tapering limbs was made up of a great swollen head with tiny eyes. Everyone on the beach gathered around to see its violet skin pulsating on the baked stone. A man picked the animal up by inserting his first two fingers into its mouth, and in a half-crouch, he lifted it and swung it over his shoulder. Then with the force of his whole arm, he beat the body down hard on the ground. Again and again, the man concentrated on nothing but raising the head and dangling legs from the ground, now sticky with ooze released by the octopus, and beating it down again, softening it for cooking.

Although we were all strong swimmers as a result of being by the sea all summer, I remember looking past the sunshine and glittering blue and throwing myself into my book instead. 'She can read all she likes in London,' my grandmother was forever saying. 'Why doesn't that child get out on that windsurf, get into the water, instead of sitting there, doing nothing with those books.' Our house in London was full of books, but more often I lay on the floor gazing at the spines (in my parents' bedroom, *Why I'm Not a Christian, O, How the Wheel Becomes It,*

Reading in the garden in Antibes

Paris is Burning, Voyage in the Dark, and downstairs, *The Crosland Diaries, 1963-67, The Crosland Diaries, 1968-75*) and repeating them to myself in a mumbled incantation that went nowhere. I hardly ever read when I could stare out of the window or pick at the carpet instead, and only read in France, when I wasn't allowed to. It was partly in silent protest at the fact that my father never came with us. What had happened to banish him from my grandparents' house I didn't know, but I took this banishing of books as a proper pastime as a veiled barb against him.

My father, at least to me, was always a palpable absence at the house. He was never invited, he never came with us and he was never mentioned. That he was a journalist and had to stay in touch with unstoppable news and press deadlines was taken as the reason he always stayed at home in London. Holidays were not considered integral to family life then; they were even a bit sneered at. It was true that he was a political commentator, who thrived on hard news and had a column to write. It became abundantly clear to me the real reason he never came with us was that he and my grandmother could not tolerate each other's presence for dinner, let alone breakfast, lunch and the rest. I saw them in the same room in our house in London maybe three times in my life. With the eyes of children trained on them, the tension felt like an unfunny comedy about to happen. Her snobbery, irrational temper and eccentric logic clashed disastrously with his discretion, his intellect and his inability to put up with people who bored him. His birthday was in the summer, some time in August. There was only one year I remember when we telephoned him from Antibes, and I remember approaching the phone with a shyness that I sensed in him too at the other end – or perhaps he was simply taken aback by the interruption, and remembered that he was talking to a child to whom he had nothing much to say. My birthday fell in the summer too and, while I had no expectations of it, it was odd that it also went largely unremarked in France. I only really noticed as I got older, and I took the reason to be that I was too much an extension of my father, so dislikeable for that. For my grandmother, the source of the problem with my father was that she was incapable of communicating with someone who was both poor and clever. In her eyes, he came from nowhere. My father seemed to make something out of nothing, and she hated him for it.

It was later, too, that I realised my grandfather stayed in the house more and more because he had emphysema. He never smoked, but the disease might have been a resurgence of the TB he had had as a child, when he was taken to the seaside once or twice. The trips were part of his parents' remedial efforts, and not to run around half-naked and jump in the sea. He only once joined us on the beach, fully clothed down to his loafers and watch.

His domain was in the house, where he gradually began to depend on oxygen cylinders. At first, he was hooked up to them only at night. Then, they began to accompany him by his side all day as well. He became more sedentary, taking his extra oxygen in through plastic tubes attached to his nose. They emanated from his large nostrils in a thin fluorescent green line, increasingly hidden in the folds of a navy-blue dressing gown he began to wear in the daytime. His breathing became more laboured, and he occasionally spat fat globules of phlegm into a jar he kept among the medicines, notepads, copies of *Paris Match* and *Private Eye*, and the bottles of Badoit by his bed.

Around him, my grandmother ran the house with the theatrical force of a spurned imperial dowager, often laying the blame for its quirks on us children, offloading this with venom onto her husband. Swinging on the gates with my sisters, we heard her shouting, '*Tricheuses! Elles sont tricheuses!*' at him, referring to us as cheats. It might have been because we had used too much bath water, but the tantrums were targeted above all at my middle sister, Milla. Milla was dark-haired, and although we are close in age and there is no question we are blood-related, her big green eyes and long eyelashes, and the fat lips she inherited from my father stood out in otherwise classical features. My grandmother's lips were thin. Perhaps lips got thinner over time, making it all the more necessary to paint them red, past caring about the way the colour bled into rivulets in the surrounding skin. Even as very young children, the intense dislike my grandmother sometimes showed towards my middle sister seemed irrational. Between ourselves, we speculated that it came out of my grandmother envying her prettiness, and this purely physical cause cut down its dimensions to something laughable. The big lips unlike the thin lips of an old-fashioned face were confirmation in my grandmother's mind of a fast and loose character, of a girl too pretty for her own good and too modern to keep up with. Here was the scapegoat she seemed to need, and who infuriated her no less for being a child and defenceless. Milla had the habit of keeping her mouth a little open, as if she were 'catching flies', as my parents teased. It looked neither like a show of contrition nor one of defensive anger, and my sister was all the more provocative to my grandmother for this reason. The unequal dynamic only seemed to perpetuate the loggerheads my grandmother appeared almost to relish as part of the daily rhythm of life.

Storming out of the house, my grandmother marched across the garden and disappeared up the dry stone steps behind the olive trees. A side gate led to a hidden path and the *château d'eau*, an enormous cylindrical cement structure with a narrow ladder leading to the top. I knew, because I had seen her do it before, that she was going to find the evidence of our profligacy with the household water by climbing up the narrow metal rungs of the ladder, sheer and perpendicular against the cement walls of this great vat. Peering into the dark pool of water and shouting to check its depth by her echo, she rattled the plunger and fiddled with its chains, muttering in confirmation of her theories about the local water supply and how delicately we needed to handle it. Then she'd be back, witnessed by us all, to deliver the triumphant words to my grandfather, pursed lips, a slight smile and a maniacal twinkle in her eyes. 'You see. You see,' came the final verdict in a bitter staccato. By this she meant, yes, it was those children's ill doing.

My grandmother had always stood a few inches taller than my grandfather, and she increasingly seemed to suck the life from him. In the face of her rages, my grand father always remained an enigma. Why did he marry her? Why did he put up with her tantrums? And with severing ties with his family? Did they have lots of affairs and, like the sinister promise on one of the record sleeves in my parents' collection, did they have a lovely war? Yet my grandmother looked after him day and night, choosing him the ripest peaches, the softest cheeses, monitoring the salt in his diet and giving him plenty of chocolate because he liked it. For his part, each year he marked her birthday in a particularly sentimental way, bringing up pink champagne from the *cave*, writing her poems and calling her *poupée* and *petite fée*. These terms of endearment, passed between two usually pragmatic yet irrational adults, delighted as much as they mystified me.

As the summers went by, the rituals of life in Antibes whittled and diminished. It was enough to keep up the daily routine for a few of us on top of my grandfather's care. The habits of a lifetime were reduced, but not wiped away. Fewer of us came; my cousins stopped staying at the same time as we did; we stopped having guests. My grandmother seemed to foster a twisty politics between people wherever she went and tempers were always short by the time we packed up our car for the long drive back to London. The subtle competition she seeded between my cousins and us drove them away some summers, which made us feel at times like the lucky insiders. My father's commitments and his independence meant there was no other shore to wash up on in the long holidays. And as my mother believed, this was family, this was tradition, and family must try to stick together as best it can. She needed to be a mother, and a daughter, and she worked hard at being a wife the rest of the time. We waved and waved from the car window as we set off down the drive, Patmanathan's face streaming with tears as he and my grandmother stood level but apart in the shade of the plane tree disappearing from view.

Now you are on the shores of the Mediterranean
Beneath the lemon trees that flower all year long
You and your friends take a boat to the water and bask
One is from Nice one from La Turbie and one is
  Mentonasque
The squid half-hidden in the deep fill you with horror
And in the seaweed fishes swim emblems of the Saviour

Lines taken from 'Zone', one of what Guillaume
Apollinaire called his poems of '*fin d'amour*', written
in 1912, when aged thirty-two, he walked heartbroken
around Paris remembering his childhood and his
youthful travels.

ENGLAND

Ifind it impossible to remember whether we deliberately did not say goodbye to my father when Mum and the three of us bundled into the car to France, or whether it was he who shunned a conventional exchange of affection like that. I can't remember the 'hellos' on our return either, just that our bedroom at the top of the house looked spacious and renewed by our absence, and soon came the satisfying feeling of putting on tights for the return to school in the autumn. My father's life was also marked by trips elsewhere: a month in China, weeks in Africa, short trips to Washington or Berlin. In his pockets were strange bank notes, like the famous dollar bills and exotic ones from Tanzania. He told me those ones were worth hardly anything, although they denoted hundreds, as Tanzania was one of the poorest countries in the world. He had odd items, like a puzzle in the shape of a tower, vaunted successor to the phenomenal Rubik's cube though it never took off, and a specially minted £2 coin the Treasury was thinking of bringing in.

A gulf of tension existed in the middle of our household and between my parents, which was passed inexplicably on to us. Given the rift between my father and my mother's side of the family, however, this almost felt like a form of solidarity knitting together the asymmetry of our immediate family of five at home. While my parents seemed to have roots in such disparate places, there were times when the two of them of them seemed made for each other. Both were green-eyed, with strong-boned faces and defined lips. My mother's face was strikingly masculine, with her 60s cropped hair and the slight hook of her nose, while my father's leanness, his dancer's legs, and big lips gave him a slightly feminine aspect – or rather, gave him a kind of beauty usually associated with women.

Though he wasn't at all bullish, there was nothing remotely fey about my father. His serve at tennis never failed to splice the air an inch above the net with a fierce velocity. He wrote about international affairs – spending most of his career on the *Financial Times* – and my mother had lived them. She had grown up moving around, going to a total of twelve schools in eight countries. In Texas and Washington, she drove a Buick at sixteen years old and the family went for Coke and hamburgers on Sundays. She hated the Dublin of peasoupers and poverty; then back in the States found herself queuing in the C queue, thinking it meant 'Caucasian', not 'Coloured'. She was a stranger in Ceauşescu's Romania, and again in the extravagance of the French embassy in Mali, where she remembered the African chef running down the hallway from the kitchen holding a whole unblemished chicken skin between his fingers, having perfected the French technique of skinning a chicken so he could roll it into a ballotine, and where they bathed outside in tin baths after dark in water heated by the day. In the car, other than French nursery rhymes, she sang Negro spirituals and the American 'polly-wolly doodle' song with the line which so shocked us, 'I jumped on a nigger 'cos I thought he was a hoss'. Golliwogs were only just being phased out from adorning the side of Robinsons jam jars then, and it was no longer endearing to call my sister, dark and curly-haired as a baby, a golliwog. My cosmopolitan mother was definitely a match for my worldly, well-travelled father.

Night after night throughout my childhood, my parents went to parties together. At embassies, the Houses of Parliament, private houses in Eaton Square and Campden Hill Gardens, they joined other journalists, diplomats, politicians, and their wives in smoke-filled rooms. My mother added to the international dimension of their friends, keeping contact with families who moved in and out of London and the world's cities every few years. The marmalade-haired lioness Margaret Thatcher was beginning to dominate everything. People said that in person, she was devastatingly beautiful, and Douglas Hurd and Michael Heseltine turned to puppy dogs in her presence. Mrs Thatcher once complimented my mother on a dress she had bought for pennies in an Indian shop-of-everything on Clapham High Street, near their first house – a bright orange cotton sequined sari tunic. Black tie was part of the weekly whirl and, at these times, my parents seemed tied to each other in an unbreakable bond. For white tie, my mother had a black organza dress, with puffed sleeves standing high from the shoulders after a starch and steam treatment. It had several skirts and white trimmings – an early 80s fright, in retrospect. They disappeared on a cloud of Cabochard perfume, my father tossing a white silk scarf over his suit. I loved the feel of the grey velvet ribbon knotted in a bow around the perfume bottle's neck, and to know that my parents were together doing what they did best.

Occasionally, if they had had a very good evening, they came back singing, or rather, my mother singing and trying to get my father to dance. He had only the most eccentric rhythm for music or dancing, but where he had an innate sense of rhythm was for language. He was completely deaf in one ear, dating from forceps applied too carelessly at his birth, and this gave him an odd gait. Often he sat in a spiral, a bit like an Otto Dix painting, crossed legs pointing one way, the opposite ear craning the other way. He would suddenly shift the angle of his head to catch something he wanted to hear, and he sometimes asked you to come and sit on his right, by his 'good ear'. This always seemed like a compliment. Though he was a very good listener, he was also good at making it clear if what you had said was boring. Maybe this part-deafness had something to do with him having more of an internal than an external rhythm to life. Unable to dance or drive or even cycle very steadily, he knew the inner beat of words. After the talk of politics – the future of the Common Market, the clash between Hurd and Heseltine in the Cabinet, the distant possibility of a single currency – out came the poetry. Great chunks of *Hamlet*, *Macbeth*, the sonnets of John Donne, their philosophical reach dissolving into the limpidity of Keats' odes, zany lines from Blake, and the ferocity of Larkin poured from his lips. It was a phenomenal ability and exhilarating to witness.

Ours was a tall, thin house, with lots of stairs and the kitchen and dining room in a low-ceilinged basement. There was little natural light down there and we used candles as well as low lamps even for lunch in the dining room. Days were very long, as we waited for my father to come home late in the evening. As soon as we were old enough to be past kitchen suppers in high chairs and having tea before bath time, we were expected to stay awake for a proper dinner. My mother clung onto this ritual as a legacy of the way she had grown up, and because if we didn't have dinner together, we would barely see each other. On Friday nights in particular, the wait for dinner seemed endless, to the extent that I sometimes fell asleep with my head on the kitchen table. My father found me there once as he swept in finally, tapping me lightly on the shoulder in a rare physical gesture. At the end of dinner, I was released to go to bed before my sisters, but fell asleep on the way up, slumped on the stairs, tired and also reluctant to go up any further on my own. Fridays were so late because he was putting the paper

to bed, a mysterious ritual engagement that took pre
cedence over putting us to bed.

My father had brilliant qualities, hailed by all his many
friends, but there was no denying that he was difficult to
live with. We left for school much earlier than he left the
house, but at weekends or half-term, the routine was plain
to see. He began to run his bath not long after he got up, but
the running of the bath with scalding-hot water went on for
some time. He went in and out of the bathroom, and up
and down the stairs repeatedly, clouds of steam following
him, all the time holding his wireless — as he called it —
and listening to the news. A battered espresso maker
containing muddy coffee perched on the outer edge of the
electric hob in the kitchen, as if this balance would prevent
it stewing into boot polish over the course of the morning.
A dark stain grew around the coffee pot – the accumulating
smell of burnt coffee is still a phantom memory – results
my father was indifferent to and didn't seem to connect
with the fact that he drank his coffee cold anyway.

During the three hours or so it took to complete these
ablutions, it was best to be at the top of the house, or
quickly down and out of the front door without inter-
cepting him on the stairs. Five newspapers came through
the door each day, and finally these were all gathered
into the steaming bathroom and my father disappeared
into his bath with them. The wireless was turned off
and he began to absorb the newspapers' contents, while
sweating out the night before. Then came the coughing

– '*tousse, tousse, tousse*' – a repeated hack best evoked in the French verb, escalating to a bronchial vomit that reverberated through the house, painful to listen to and alarming for any friends who came to stay. Eventually, he was dressed and gone, to return late, if he or both my parents weren't going out to one of their parties.

Without fail, the day ended for him late at night, long after the rest of us had gone off to bed. He seemed to sleep only in the lost part of the night where the latest and earliest hours meet, surrounded by the submerged tracts of other people's dreams, when only Father Christmas was about, if you believed in that sort of thing. If he was home, the process began by his walking around the drawing room with a drink in hand, a straight-sided tumbler of pebbled glass and distinctly 70s appearance. They were one of his few possessions. He had the barest equipment needed to go into the world; the rest was my mother's. If he had owned more himself, my mother had in all like-lihood phased them out as atrocities against good taste. We haven't thrown those glasses away, but stashed them at the back of the cupboard and I still can't bear to look at them now. The way they half hid their pungent amber-coloured contents inside the thick textured glass sits them in another era, one that is finished now.

Our house was full of loose floorboards, the sound of which, as anyone who has lived in an old house knows, carries strangely and can indicate where a person is two floors below them. As he paced across them giving away the familiar creaks, I knew he'd come to a standstill to light a cigarette. In a curious gesture, he lifted his elbow high above his ear while his fingers brought the cigarette to his lips. The first puff was a fierce and noisy inhalation, far longer than normal lungs could put up with. Then it was released in a great plume, just as noisy, as the arm holding the cigarette stretched and wavered up above his head, tendons palpably relaxing from the nicotine, the fingers, hand and arm limbering up for work. And he was off into his study, a small room on the landing dominated by his desk. Cigarette smoke curled around the door, and the sound of his writing for the deadline the following day commenced. Like gunfire, the typewriter keys banged, short bursts followed by long ones, then short again.

Sometimes the disparity between how other people knew him, and the values he showed to the world, and how he behaved to us at home was extremely distressing. I say 'values', but this was among the forbidden words, an example of the meaningless, pretentious sort of sloppy thinking be abhorred. The same went for the word 'opinion', too woolly and conceited, much better expressed by the neutral word 'view'. Others were 'quite' unless used as a complete sentence; this vague indication of degree was intolerable, as something either was or was not like something else, although he often liked to comment on a 'grey area'. 'Highbrow' and 'lowbrow' showed a slavish way of thinking – a distinctly middlebrow way. The only brow worth defining was the middlebrow as this exemplified the senseless labelling of anything abstract as high or low. 'Hopefully' was out as a solecism, though the German word '*hoffentlich*' was acceptable. He steered us against the word 'hate' too. 'Hate is a very strong word,' he would say in a mild tone, asking if that is what we really meant. Swearing was 'meaningless' and the resort of people with 'no imagination'; I still find it difficult to swear now.

Worst of all was to make an assertion using the words, 'I feel'. Only thinking was allowed, not feeling. But his words 'Come on', a pause and 'think', often came across as friendly, as if this was the only game worth playing. At an event given at the Bank of England, where an elite of journalists, economists and business leaders were gathered, Robin Leigh-Pemberton rounded up his speech with words along the lines of 'And in view of these events, the Bank of England feels...' to which my father interjected, 'Does the Bank of England *feel*?' to a chorus of hoots and 'here-heres'. Infuriatingly in an argument, as our voices pitched louder and higher, he would counter with the quiet words 'Go on', challenging us to develop our arguments and see if we could remain reasonable, while he steadfastly refused ever to raise his voice. It was provocative and exasperating in equal measure. There were times when we hated it through our tears, and others when we exulted in the independence of mind we saw, eventually, that it could give us.

Because of his polished and articulate delivery, cheekbones jutting, arm demarcating the point with dancing fingers, it may have seemed imperious to some people if he interjected like this. He was unusually determined to clarify a point, but it was a misreading to think he was pompous. More often he acted like an icebreaker, reminding us to throw in a joke and not to get too sucked into too partial a view of things. Of all the criticisms, being pompous was highest on the list, along with taking yourself too seriously. One person's intellectual could often be a 'pseud' to him – his pseud-detector was second to none. This sort of posturing and pretension was likely only to land you looking 'too small for your boots'. He levelled the same judgments at us children as at anyone else, and could mostly get away with it because it was far more compelling to believe him than not to accept what he said. He was usually right, and if not, at least he was never boring.

It was harder then, when he rejected our small gestures. In my first year at the Lycée, my four-year-old cousin and I were very friendly and very competitive, but I knew absolutely that my painting of a Christmas tree was the best one. I brought it into the drawing room to show my father late in the evening, but he was reading so I left it on the chair. The next day, I came back to find it thrown in the bin. Acting on the family trait of obstinacy, I pulled it out again and tried to uncurl its brittle painted surface, but the fury with which my father crossed the room to remove it from his space beat me back into the doorway and I didn't try it again.

Of all the most reprehensible forms of behaviour, being pompous and patronising was the one he considered worst of all. Given the sophistication of many of his arguments, this is perhaps surprising – paradoxical, even. He had decided somewhere along the way never to patronise us children, always speaking in an even voice, not hesitating to tell us where we had gone wrong, and keen to show us the nuances where we had assumed it was black and white. Cute derivations and the singsong voice did not come at all naturally to him. He never used complicated words for the sake of it, however. He was a journalist above all, and the need to make a point as lucidly as possible in as few words as possible, while entertaining your reader, was pressing. The unintended consequence was that what he said was often beyond us – but far more inspiring than the opposite extreme of parenting at least, even though it took some figuring out to reach this conclusion. I had the sense of missing him long before he died, and somehow always felt as though I were walking in this long shadow.

After a short time in the house in Clapham, where both my sisters lived as babies, my parents managed to buy the house I grew up in, in Notting Hill. I was brought there aged under a year from Denmark, where my mother had retreated to her parents, heavily pregnant and knowing that the third time around she would get no hands-on help from my father. She and the babies had a far more comfortable time of it at the French embassy in Copenhagen. There, things were done in pomp. My cousin and I were due on very similar dates – I was born on 10th July, and she was born on 14th July – so my grandfather flew the French flag above the embassy early that year. It was raised four days before Bastille Day for my birth, and then stayed up for the birth of another granddaughter and the party on the night of 14th. Emma was taken to the Danish nursery in one of the embassy cars, and Milla was bathed in a washbasin, powder-puffed and perfumed in one of the many gilt-mirrored bathrooms. The embassy wasn't typically equipped for babies, so I slept in a large fish kettle. A fish kettle with the French flag flying above, along with the line 'you were born in a palace', were the stories I heard from my mother about my infancy – the kind of things that little girls like to hear, maybe, but I didn't latch onto them much, as they bore no relation to my life. They struck me instead as a distant echo of the life my grandparents led before us. My mother didn't have much choice except to stay with her parents while she was having the third of three babies, but she was starting to gain the uncomfortable sense of being caught between the demands of two opposing sides of her family.

The house my parents had bought in London was almost impossible to raise children in. It had no modern plumbing and barely any floorboards. My mother had to deal with it, so she bundled up the three of us and went back to her husband as soon as she could. In any case, she was carrying out a plan that her parents had a role in. They had not seen the new house, but they had navigated its purchase from afar. My grandmother was gravely concerned that their daughter, and she herself, should boast a smarter address in central London, even if the house was in need of total renovation.

An old lady called Miss Hubbard had lived and died in the house and its corners still held her forgotten possessions: a set of cut-glass perfume bottles with silver lids, a Minton chamber pot with a rose design, a Bible box stamped with black letters reading 'The Rvd Hubbard' that served almost as a coffee table except for the crack across its heavy lid. Where my parents put their bathroom was an open landing with a window over the garden. Next to this was a water closet – a tiny room containing space only for a Corinthian column made of mahogany inset with a lift-up seat and a chain attached to a brown pipe snaking up to the ceiling. In the smallest room at the top, which became my room when I was about twelve, old Miss Hubbard's nephew had lived. He was lame, so the Victorian wooden bedstead that was left behind when we moved in came with a metal crank attached for lifting his body and reclining him again. The room had also contained a commode, a high-backed wooden armchair with a bench that lifted up on hinges to reveal a stained receptacle. The boy had not lived far into adulthood, and when he died Miss Hubbard was left without any family. Neighbours said they used to hear her calling for him out of the top window and over the spread of gardens presided over by the sycamore tree at the end of ours. When we were small, old Miss Hubbard seemed vividly present in the house. Pushed to it, my mother admitted sensing draughts or a door slamming when it shouldn't, and my father was not as impervious to these theories as he seemed from a distance. In different ways, they were both believers in magic.

We had very few photographs in our house, and neither of my parents was handy with a camera. Two of these few photographs were of strangers. One of them was of a stern upstanding fellow in a dog collar – the Reverend Hubbard presumably and a relative of old Miss Hubbard. The other was a modern framed photograph that sat on the bookshelves in my father's study. The words Herr Malcolm Rutherford were inscribed on its frame, but it contained a picture not of my father but of somebody else, a pleasant-looking man who apparently was a colleague of my father's from his time in Germany before I was born. I knew this from asking my mother, as it seemed so odd to have only one photograph on display and that not of a family member, and not of anybody we knew. If my father was out, I often picked this framed picture up to experience the same bafflement as to why he had it, and seemed to have no others. His study was extremely neat, the surface of his desk always in the same sparse forma-tion of leather blotter and blank notepad, pen pot with three pens in it, ashtray, cigarette box, lamp. There was barely anything I could find by looking, nothing to elaborate on his non-professional character, his indulgences or obsessions or collections.

But among the analytical volumes, the political diaries and the staple-bound bulletins of think-tanks, there was one book on the shelf that I found and liked very much. It was one of the Gallimard editions, in its familiar white livery, black lettering and gold-tooled spine. There was a simple line drawing of a man's face on the front. It was an unmistakably Gallic profile, as I had generalised that in my mind, hook-nosed and pensive, with upwards-sloping eyes giving off a philosophic air above a squiggle of pipe

there was the rocker, a wooden hemisphere in which we could clamber and seesaw, making like sailors or stowaways. Further back, where the sycamore tree that would be split in two by the 1987 storm cast its shadow on laurel and elderflower, the rope ladder swing hung. It caused what seemed my last childhood accident, the first time I stopped crying at the point when I realised it wasn't that bad, even though my mother made a drama out of the scar where I gashed my leg on a jagged branch in the path of the swing. Our cat often jumped from nowhere to sit on the window ledge of my father's study, licking her paws or eyeing the movement of birds. I was vaguely jealous, both of the cat and of him, when he opened his study window to let her in. Even though he didn't seem to court it, our cat seemed to have a special relationship with him, coming to curl her back and tail around his legs as he sat at the head of the table after dinner finishing his wine, or interrupting his work to jump through his window and consider taking a nap in the pool of warmth beneath his desk lamp.

The Gallimard book I found in my father's study was called simply *Guillaume Apollinaire*. In it, the poem I had repeated with my grandfather about the best home containing a woman, a cat, books and friends was set in an illustration of just this, a cat dominating a private scene with a lamp, flowers and books. The style of the picture reminded me not just of the house in Antibes, the pictures there and in the Picasso museum, with the simple hand that was modern and primitive at the same time, but also of my mother's pictures. If she had had to give up the chance of doing much else with three babies arriving in the space of thirty-six months, when we were small she did keep up her painting. Once a week, she went off to Whitechapel with a flamboyantly eccentric neighbour, in a brown spotted garment that had also served as a maternity dress. Under her arm was a thickly paint-splattered wooden box containing tubes in a specialist rainbow of umber, burnt sienna, cyan, magenta and ochre, and palette knives almost as soft as foil. It baffled me that my mother's portraits never bothered with the detail of faces or hands, giving only the characteristic shape of people against blocks of colour and stylised flowers. The photographs in the Gallimard book, this bilingual store of scraps, jottings and text I mostly couldn't understand, showed paintings with a family resemblance to my mother's, looking remarkably feral next to the men in suits.

This book seemed to contain a promise, a channel into the past and to places I knew or would have known if I had been born then, but it also blocked me with its mysteries. I didn't know the people inside it, though I felt the familiarity of them and of some of the places they lived and passed through. Its bilingualism was also strange, though French was my mother's first language and my father spoke German well. Looking through the pages, I saw something I thought I understood but could not hold in my hand. It confirmed a type of life I thought was lived by my parents and their friends before I was born, and gestured to things I wanted to find out.

Bedtime stories with my father were rare, so the occasions he read to us were filled with expectation. They collapse into one memory, a single scene of us walking upstairs together, up and up, and the well of the staircase opening out into a realm of possibility. I remember almost bursting with a plenitude of happiness – I must have been around three or four years old, following the Pied Piper up the stairs in a jaunty trance. Sitting on his lap, my ear was at the height of his heart and lungs, and the few memories of listening to the crackle of his breath as he prepared to read to us bring back a magical promise of revelation. The wheeze in his smoke-scorched throat seemed to add to the depth of what he was about to bring to life, the secrets he was about to impart. He began with the names of the three little girls – our names – who lived in the house Peter Pan used to come to at night. Looking out across the wooden bars that protected us from the windows at the top of the house, I could see the treetops swaying at the corner of the street and darkness gathering in readiness for the adventures beyond. From behind those trees, Peter Pan, the boy who was brilliant but never wanted to grow up, might appear at any moment, flying through the window. Perhaps now he was spying on pirates from the hollow of the tree trunk in Kensington Gardens.

My father seemed to have genuine empathy for the conundrum in which Peter Pan was trapped, going on brilliant escapades but always being a boy, forever whirling around the same games and failing to understand the sophistication and subtleties of Wendy, who would inevitably leave him behind one day. His voice was never too loud but its timbre was rich and commanded attention. I glimpsed for a moment the acceptance behind his eyes that to be a boy forever would be stultifying, but to grow up was painful, and that life was full of these flawed exchanges.

More often, my father didn't come upstairs with us, but we occasionally sat next to each other on the sofa to read aloud. This piece of furniture was always known in our house as a *canapé*, and this term encoded so much about the differences between the two sides of the family. All things material and to do with material taste came from the French side, my mother's side. My father's life was marked by a minimum of possessions. The two sides of my parents' bed were a study of their differences; hers laden with thick paperbacks, creams and pill pots, pens, Carambar wrappers, the telephone. Hers also had at its foot a velvet-tasselled footstool on which sat the television. The fat dimensions of this black and white set framed a diminutive screen; a round wheel located the channels with frustrating inaccuracy. His side was bare except for a box of man-size tissues and a plug-in clock, not digital but of utilitarian 70s design. Though this sparseness of stuff on my father's side was always apparent, when he died I was still shocked by the few things that he left to show where he had been: a single pen pot on his desk, the unlined white pad that was always blank at the end of each day, yesterday's words in print today and gone tomorrow; his ashtray, a greenish block of rock crystal, scooped out with a perfect hemisphere of empty space.

Where these two sides converged was in a half-articulated scorn for matters of straightforward comfort. At no time could any of us throw ourselves onto the couch, cuddle up on the settee, bounce on the sofa, fall asleep on the cushions. Instead we sat next to each other on the *canapé*, where we might read aloud together. Children grab at any semblance of a game, of fun, contest and story-telling. So we made a game of guessing who my father was quoting – the three of us usually shouting 'Shakespeare!'

My sisters and I

and we're supposed to go to sleep. I had some marbles in my pocket, and I took them out and I was playing with them on the table, and then I dropped one and it made a noise. So Madame Janvier told me to sit on the floor at the front of the class. And she confiscated my marbles.'

Later, this episode took a grander twist in that I didn't just drop the marble; I threw it at the window, making a really impressive noise. 'Why did you do that?' my father asked with the same equanimity. He didn't seem in the least bothered I had caused a disruption and not done what I was supposed to do and everybody else was doing. He was only curious as to why. 'Because I wanted to see what it was like to be *punie*,' I said. Madame Janvier's son Guillaume, because he was a little bit younger than the class, slept on a bed by the side of her desk, and I wanted to see what it was like over there, near him. But I didn't try to explain all that, to myself or to him. My father loved this story, and repeated it often, using his bad French accent to say that word 'punished' in French as I had said it, making it sound more like 'poo-nee'. There was something about the objective desire to see what it was like to break a rule that appealed to him. The bilingual twist only added to this, as if states of being might be experienced differently in different languages. That rules can be arbitrary, and are 'made to be broken', and that censorship was a form of prejudice, informed his minimal notion of parental discipline. It seemed to take a long time before I was able to impress him as much with anything else.

Fantastic atolls
of revolvers what
a taste
for liv
ing Ah !

Multicoloured lak..
in solar glaciers

1 very
small
bird
that hasn't any
tail and
that flies off
when you
give him
o ne

tiny carpets of taste let's foam obscure sounds
and your mouth its breath
of azure

hear hear the cry footsteps pho
NOGRAPH hear hear THE ALOE
bursts open and the tiny flute

'Eventail des saveurs', 'Fan of Flavours' or 'Flavourscape'
is one of the experiments in visual poetry Apollinare
called his 'calligrammes'. They are both playful and
typographically precise – this one resembles a face.
He wrote most of them during the war period, and this
one serves as a secret love poem, and as marvellous
relief from the darkening days of combat far from the
people he loved.

FRANCE

As a small child, my mother was left in Paris with a family who looked after her and took her to her convent school each morning, while her parents went off to live in Dublin. She had done very well at school so far, despite bullying by some of the sisters who ran the place. At first, she was picked up each afternoon and taken home to be stuffed with jam *tartines* by my competitive grandmother, fearful of being upstaged by a slim daughter, and stories at bedtime from her father. Then her parents' next post came and they decided to leave her behind, along with the next child, her brother Mark, affectionately known as Markie-too – except that he was left with a different family, closer to the school that he went to. Weeks into this arrangement, the schoolwork of both declined, they stopped listening in class and couldn't sleep. They were so miserable, it was like an illness, and the schools and families looking after the two children contacted their parents to come and get them. My mother remembers weeping as she waved goodbye to Madame Avérousse, who had looked after her as if she were her own for months, and this woman weeping too as she waved back to the little girl as she disappeared into a large car with her parents. My grandmother had never been so soft and emotional, but still she was my mother's mother, not a paid stand-in, and her daughter — my mother — loved and missed her for that.

The pattern continued all through my mother's child-hood; she was left alone at schools and in cities where she was a stranger. Her father kept on being posted to bigger and better places, and her mother had no romantic ideas about staying at home and passing up a life of glamour and adventure elsewhere. Occasionally, though, as a small child, my mother and her parents joined a huge extended family for the holidays, at her grandparents' home in the countryside near Lyon. This was where my grandfather and his big family were from, and the house that I heard about called Les Vallières. My mother was the eldest of her siblings, and in the early years relations with their father's family were still functional. They stopped visiting by the time her younger brothers were walking. There were nine sets of aunts and uncles, giving her twenty-seven cousins to play with, some of them looking remarkably like her, her father and her little brothers. A fountain in the court-yard of the château sprayed jets of water that was pumped across from land belonging to another house they had, not far across the border in Switzerland where the moun-tain water was reputed to be so tonic. This is where they collected extra supplies of water when the whole family came to stay, and when the weather was warm enough to undertake the annual washing of vast piles of linen. Sheets were spread over the fields and hedges to dry. My mother was once shocked to walk into one of the back rooms near the kitchen to find a vat of boiling water and a woman pounding and swirling a heavy vortex of cloth in it. A smell of rust or iron clung to the damp suds in the air, and rows and rows of nappy-like cloths were hung up on lines to dry, some of them still streaked with pale brownish stains.

The château was self-sufficient, except for rice, chocolate, tea and coffee. My grandfather did not eat food at his family's table that was not produced from their own land until he left to do his military service. Chocolate came from the family's factory in Lyon, and at Christmas time they merchandised a chocolate called *Réveillon*, for the feast on Christmas Eve when everybody stayed up all night, famished after midnight mass, eating oysters followed by calf's kidneys, followed by capon, endives braised in white wine, beans in fine sauces, cheeses, tarts, crystallised fruit, chocolate, nougat, nuts. In the First World War, the château had been taken over by the German army. Upstairs, the bedroom doors each carried a plaque engraved with a German name, Colonel von Fritzdorf, Colonel Brandt, Lieutenant von Hesselbach. The master of the house, my grandfather's father, who had lived through two wars with the Germans and anticipated a third, had decided never to remove them. It was 'a lesson in humility'.

The children played outside, and depending on the time of year, foraged for mushrooms in the woods or picked berries from bushes. Croquet was spread out on the lawn, they swam in the stream at the bottom of the garden and children and adults lost to each other at tennis. At the end of the holidays, the children all dressed up to put on a play. Chairs were assembled on the terrace, garlands wound through the balustrade, rocking horses wheeled out and decorated with borrowed silk ties and lace-frilled dressing gowns. The children wore Pierrot outfits, riding breeches, tall Merlin hats and organza dresses so they could sport as farmers, huntsmen, elves and fairies. At the end they lined up in order of height to sing a song in as close a harmony as they could manage.

It seemed a mad idea, and it was, but my grandparents wanted to create their own new château in the countryside, near rivers and woods, away from the bustle of Paris and the heat and storms of the Midi. Paris and the Côte d'Azur were the classic poles of their way of life. They had owned a house in Antibes from when my mother and her brothers were little, even though they lived away from it in the States for a fifteen-year stretch. With my grandfather retired and no longer travelling, a château in the country was a new project for them. One year, in the holidays when I was five or six, instead of going all the way down south, we drove halfway down France, stopping only when we came to a tiny village in the Loire valley. It was pouring with rain. There could not have been a night more suited to getting lost outside the village, and finding at last a high stone wall we suspected was the right one.

We followed this wall enclosing layers of chestnut and poplar trees and we did not know what beyond, until we reached an imposing set of gates. Obscured by the rain that made these trees grow so abundantly and the earth give off its smell of moss and leaf, the grey painted gates were lit up long enough by a flash of lightning for us to stop and try them. It was the château, abandoned and empty, where we camped on folding beds and heated water from a kettle on the floor.

In daylight, the façade was a typical French pale grey, with tall shutters at intervals, floor to ceiling at ground level and getting smaller on higher floors. Central steps led to double wooden doors with a statue of a veiled lady in an alcove above them. The ground floor was a series of large, echoing interconnecting rooms, with kitchens at either end. It made no difference to us whether we appointed those or any of the other rooms as kitchens, as all they offered were deep stone troughs and unreachably tall cupboards it was impossible to imagine storing food in. The corners hung with spider webs, and every surface was covered in mouse droppings and dead flies. The central rooms had facing walls lined with mirrors, which exaggerated the effect of a Russian doll-like trap. It became the setting of a recurring nightmare I had, in which I was left alone in one of these rooms. There was always the garden and fields beyond the shutters, but whatever time of day, the empty interior was cold and shadowed by these paint-blistered slats and I don't remember ever looking out through clear glass or open windows.

Up the winding stairs, the wood was smooth and recessed from the passage of many footsteps. The château had been used in the past as a school, and in the attics were a few remnants of the institution that had taken life there once. Scattered metal trays with compartments for different food items provided a drab reflection of how children had once had lunch in a refectory located somewhere in the building. In the low-ceilinged rooms on the top floor, the narrow geometry of old casement windows reduced the outside world to a slice of grass and sky. Up there in the attics, I had the sensation of time collapsed, sound expelled from this interior zone, nothing left. It was a necessary ritual to raid its every corner, looking for nothing and finding nothing. My mother took some of the old board shutters to paint on 'one day when I have nothing to do'. It was safer to clatter all the way down again, past the empty rooms and the single unplumbed bath on clawed feet that we never tried to use, out into the open space and the possibilities of roaming the land, seeing the estate anew with the distortions of distance.

I was always in London when I had the dream of being alone in the abandoned rooms within rooms, but over there in the daytime, with no thought for what the adults were up to, we explored. Although I knew the sea, it was my first experience of the countryside. In one lost corner, on the edge of thicker wooded terrain, was a clutter of stone headlands, each not much higher than my knee.

Rising at chaotic angles from a thick moss, these deep-grey stones looked something like weathered old graves, but were uninscribed and too irregularly shaped. Whorls of lichen marked them, whispering subterranean secrets at me, reminding me of the patterns on the rocks where the waves kept pulling me back as I clambered to shore in the South. They seemed partway between gravestones and more ancient objects, stellae or glyphs, but there were no runes or traditions I knew to interpret them as pagan offerings. The stones hovered somewhere between functional and symbolic while being neither.

My grandparents had underestimated the vast expense of the overhaul it would need to render the château functional and to run it after that. Nevertheless, it sat on acres of land, scattered over which were plenty of dependencies, the *maison du gardien*, the stables, the orangery. For years, we went there whenever possible, over the Easter holidays and sometimes dividing the summer holidays between the château and the South. Swept up in my grandmother's vision and her incessant energy for fixing, remaking and planning, we were her shoemaker's elves. Between two cars, our battered Ford and my grandmother's Renault, we packed up food, clothes and tools and drove to one or the other, the women drivers in convoy. My grandfather sat in the passenger seat wearing his *casquette*, and we zipped Chloé, the cat, into a sausage bag. I tried to arrange it so that her head popped out of the opening and the bag served as her special car seat.

My grandfather outside the orangery

But she hated the drive and spent it crouched in a silent bundle as if ready to pounce if it weren't for being encased in somebody's old weekend bag. Whiskers downturned, she monitored the situation from a small plastic window at one end that was conveniently part of the bag's design.

We moved into the orangery, itself a large enough building with two wings. One wing of it was the orangery itself, the south-facing inner wall of it set almost entirely with glass panes to bring in maximum sunshine and light. The room had a giant stone fireplace at one end, and was painted at the other end with murals of a village street scene with a lonely fox-like dog pointing its nose in the air. It was large enough to make a sitting-room area by the fireplace, have a billiard table at the other end and a dining table and chairs we moved around at random. The other wing had a long corridor running along it and off that, adjoining rooms with bathrooms in between the bedrooms. Each of them looked into the central space through glass doors, onto a deep square swimming pool. In our time there, the swimming pool was full of dark rainwater where salamanders, frogs and newts had long been spawning and big black beetles paddled the surface.

Still, we tried to tame some of the garden and the fields and woodland. My grandmother set us to work as her team, handing each of us children a rake and a pair of 'hands', two bits of wooden plank we used to pick up mounds of dead leaves and twigs and toss them on the bonfire. We were sent into the fields to gather hay, raking heaps of it into bundles. We pulled up the brambles and small trees that would interfere with the pathways they were planning and tried to lie them in clever shapes against the bonfires. The old wooden window frames needed sugar-soaping and repainting, the glass panes needed to be cleaned, and the tiled floor perpetually swept with the handmade witches' brooms we had for the purpose.

The boundary between inside and outside was thin, but in the orangery we made this a virtue. Although we colonised the building, it was always a hinterland between outdoor living and furnished shelter. Using tree stumps, we set up trestle tables and benches outside, avoiding the trunks that had turned almost as soft as the terraces of grey fungus growing from their swollen rain-pelted grain. At lunchtime, we brought trays and baskets of food from the orangery kitchen, and sat eating *saucisson*, mortadella, lentil salad, radishes, *celery rave*, bread and cheese, kicking our legs in long grasses. For dessert, we had greengages from the trees. It was my grandfather's idea not just to remove brambles and nettles and raze the hay, but also to plant a young sapling for each of us. Ringed around with chicken wire, they were about as tall as us and feathered with pale leaves. My grandfather had not seen his own brothers and sisters in years, and wanted to create a new continuity in the grounds of this château in the Loire, full of echoes of the past but without personal history. If those saplings survived, they would now be several times our height and of unbending thickness.

Raking was taken seriously by my grandmother; it was essential for the upkeep of gravel drives and all parts of the garden. It meant putting your elbow into it, rigorously driving it over the ground, careful not to dislodge the even spread of gravel or sand, and stopping often, but not too often, to push handfuls of dead leaves from its prongs. If I handled the rake with any weakness, she might grab it from my hands and give it a sarcastic whirl to illustrate the 'niminy-piminy' way I had done it. I fleetingly imagined my father trying to cooperate in this regime. My mother only once — in passing — mentioned that the single time he had stayed in the South with his parents-in-law, before

I was born, their 'setting him to work' spelt the beginning of the end. The phrase was enough to tell the story; it was one layer of their total distaste for each other. What made us reluctant to linger on this was the way it cast both sides in an absurd light, and my father in a slightly pathetic one too. In his view, gardens were to sit in and read, and otherwise ignore unless mediated through words – Marvell's 'green thought in a green shade'. He was never known for being physically practical. His pale northern skin could not tolerate the brutal open sunlight of the South. His introspection did not court it. But what grown person of any reason would put up with being bullied as to the correct stance in holding a garden tool, and set to clear somebody else's dead leaves to an inscrutable standard of perfection? I accidentally opted out one day when I woke up pale and shaking with exhaustion, fell on my breakfast in a ravenous frenzy, then threw it all up and passed out until dinner time. In general, though, my sisters and I were good at and good for the tasks my grandmother set us.

This was all part of my grandmother's resourcefulness and her leadership. She had adopted France along with her husband, and left the relative provincialism of her childhood behind her. In her eyes, anyway, it was provincial. She seemed always to push further than the hand that was dealt her. She became a pupil at Cheltenham Ladies' College as a result of writing to the school herself to ask for a place. When her parents sent her for a season in Paris aged eighteen, instead of to Cambridge like her brother, that was the beginning and the end of her scorn for her family. She found a husband, joined the army and never looked back. 'Come follow, follow, follow, follow me, Whither shall I follow follow follow?' she sang in an impressive scale, and we followed on her marching heels across fields and woodland. Once we had gathered a serious amount of hay, we went and paid a visit to the neighbouring farmer. She negotiated the exchange of hay we had collected for riding lessons. We were fully aware of her charisma then. The three of us learned how to mount a horse and canter around the ring of sand the farmer kept for lessons. Although I was eight, ten or even older, and had been clearing the fields with my rake and poking the bonfire, they called me '*petite mouche*' – I was an irritation like a little fly landed on the back of the horse.

My grandmother was at her best setting us projects like these, and sometimes they were dedicated to pure fun. We made a chariot from old planks and wheels, using string to pull each other along on it, and hired bicycles from the village. We found a strange bower made of metal painted black standing among the trees. It had a pointed roof, but was otherwise open to the elements, its sides made of square windows and a doorway waiting to be twined with honeysuckle. Not knowing what we could best use it for, we moved it about, lifting three corners and spinning it forward so it stabbed the ground ahead, then running round to its other side to do the same. It was good for make-believe and I remember being on my own in this bower, too old to make-believe otherwise. 'We're painting the roses red, we're painting the roses red,' I rabbited on, 'I'm late, I'm late, for a very important date.' It helped to keep slightly on the alert, in case the summons came from my grandmother to carry out one of her tasks — tying knots with small fingers, or fetching things was a common one. Sent to get the gardening gloves and secateurs from the château, I grabbed my bike and pelted off on one of the paths through woodland. All the time I suspected the task might be an impossible one; there were no gloves or secateurs or she had put them somewhere else. She always did that, hid things in impossible places or forgot where she had put them, insisting we go and get them as if only a blind or a very stupid person couldn't see where they were.

I was stewing over this as I pounded the pedals of my bike, but still forcing myself to go faster and faster in case when I got back, my grandmother's good humour had turned and she would round on me. 'Where have you been? What were you doing? I told you lunch was at one o'clock,' as a thin-lipped smile settled on her face. My hand went to my mouth automatically, in a nervous finger-biting gesture, always forgetting the swipe across the lips for this. 'Take those filthy fingers out of your mouth!' came her shriek. Then, as if she'd been truly wronged and disappointed in her estimation of the usefulness of her grandchildren, she'd let out a long series of '*Ah, la la la la la la la la la laaaaa,*' accompanied by a weary whistle of breath. In anticipation of being the butt of this ritual blaming again, I cycled faster and faster, but at the same time in furious irritation because I knew the gloves were never there in the first place. And where could I find them, somewhere in or outside of the rambling château? All of a sudden, I stopped, just before running over a mouse. It was already dead, its body a brown sac caved in on itself, its teeth bared in the way that was said to happen if an animal had rabies. I abandoned my mission and turned back, but by the time I got back to the orangery garden, they had forgotten I had gone in the first place.

The room at the corner of the orangery, connecting one wing to another and leading to the bedrooms, became a study. In the middle of it sat a campaign desk – two pillars of drawers with a leather-backed top carried by brass handles. As we raked and swept and built fires outside, occasionally threatening each other with a dip in the black pool, my grandfather sat at this desk with his books, magazines and blue-covered exercise books filled with *papiers à carreaux*. One year, after he had become very sick and rarely moved from his room, my grandmother gave one of her dramatic sighs, and in a fond moment reported him as saying, 'The only time I ever feel completely at peace is when I am at my desk.' She said it almost as if to herself, and it made a deep impression on me at the time. She had so little natural sympathy for being that way, and so rarely showed the tenderness to accept it in others. It echoed with me like the ghost of an experience I hadn't yet had, but it was only later I came to understand why.

Sitting on the ledge outside the glass-paned doors, I spent a lot of time with my middle sister examining the curious red-and-black-backed beetles crawling across the stone in single file. I could see my grandfather through the window, breathing with a whistling sound through his mouth, his chest sometimes rising forcefully and then stilling. When the others went out, I could see Chloé come out from hiding to jump on my grandfather's desk and patter her mountain paws with possessive indifference over his open books, requiring attention now the coast was clear. I followed her inside and we'd set about removing the burrs caught in her long fur. Her stomach, where the fur was pale grey and white, was clustered with these dried brown seedlings in matted tufts. But if we cleared them away and stroked her smooth, there were also ticks, which neither of us wanted to remove, protruding from the secret white skin at the roots of her fur. Hard grey sacs, smooth and leathery, ballooned from pairs of teeth sunk into her flesh, all the while filling their bodies up with her blood. This was when we felt her true form, the liquid bones beneath her thick fur. She leapt from our grasp, back into the woods to prowl unsuccessfully for mice and birds and come back covered in burrs again.

Of their four children, my grandparents strongly favoured one of their sons, their third child. He had classic good looks and was destined to be the one who followed in his father's footsteps in the French embassy, or rather in France's most strategic embassies around the world. It was for him that the château was destined, because their special son 'needed to have somewhere to entertain his friends'. The orangery increasingly became his country house. Adrift on its surfaces otherwise scattered with baskets brimming with pliers, funnels, tins of oil and balls of string were solid gold ornamental birds from Nigeria, cigars from Cuba and red lacquer boxes from Moscow. First thing some mornings, but not before my uncle had drunk a litre of coffee from a thimble-sized cup and smoked several filterless Gitanes, the neighbouring farmer came to call on him. They knocked back a few doses of the local *eau de vie* and set off on the tractor to discuss how they were going to remodel the land. The rustic setting did not stop the usual rules being observed, however: vodka on the rocks at a quarter to eight, then dinner at eight o'clock; hair always worn up in the evening and skirts to the knee. Looking over his tanned Gallic nose, my uncle might give a nod of approval as to how we'd turned out, albeit it with an ironic smile, or adding an incisive gesture to indicate where improvements could be made. He was a man who took aggressive comfort in his own skin. The clear light blue of his eyes seemed rightly to belong to a faraway child. To me, he pulled back his lips and waved his hand near his mouth, nodding to my mother. This meant I needed my teeth filed so they were smoothly shaped and did not bear the bumpy edges of a pre-adolescent's teeth.

After dinner, leaning back in his chair, if all had gone

according to plan, having supervised the cooking with his Nigerian butler, Innocent, my uncle began to hold forth on the things he loved. 'I love candles,' he said, sweeping his hand operatically across the glow given by the cande-labra. He looked at us as if testing us with any awareness of the abstruse knowledge he was imparting. 'I love wine, I love crystal, I love silver, I love clean napkins, I love

poetry, and jazz, I love billiards and cards, I love beautiful women.' We squirmed slightly in our chairs, as it seemed this outpouring of the things he loved showed no sign of stopping. He delivered his speech with an ironic and arrogant glimmer around his eyes, but there was a hard defiance behind them. It was clear the required response was absolute gravity, as a sign of respect for the master in his domain and his excellent taste. I could let out no expression. The stillness except for the candle flames would be broken and the carafes and decanters on the table, hovering with water and wine, might shatter. He only had the power to release us from the ritual worship of ritual at his table.

The tragedy of his life, other than the split that eventually divided our family once and for all, was that my uncle was not allowed to marry the woman he loved. He needed a wife to follow him around at the Ministry, to keep a beautiful house, give parties and look the part. But the one he chose was a Russian woman. Katya was beautiful in a more elaborate way than we had ever seen. She wore floor-length mink and her hair was streaked with chestnut, auburn and gold, like the markings of an Abyssinian cat. Between her sumptuous hem and her high heels, her ankles looked as brittle as ice cubes. She was extremely friendly to us, but after faithfully appearing for several years and politely facing down the disapproval of my grandparents, she was finally banished. Not only did she not have enough money, but she was '*moche comme tout'* and frankly, so it was said behind my uncle's back, she was *'immontrable, insortable'*. It was a sacrifice he made in order to retain the favour of his parents and to wait out for the right wife and companion to his career as a diplomat. But that wife, who could be loved by him and accepted by his parents, never came along.

He fared incomparably better than his older brother though. Markie was rarely included in any of these gatherings. He lived in Paris on his own; nobody seemed too bothered about where. He was a university professor, and once a year sent one of his essays to his mother to read. She took it from her bag as if it were a curious knitting pattern she might tackle over coffee after lunch, greeting it with high-pitched titters about the sort of fiendish knot her son had designed to trap her in. 'He is so clever, it's in*fu*-*ri*ating! My godfathers. He's read everything! Everything before 1600!' He specialised in Medieval Literature, fitting work for him to be typecast and ridiculed as the family oddball. But the ostracising and criticism began when he was a baby, and everything from his needing glasses to his using his left hand to brush his teeth – a sure sign of his deviancy – would be verbally fired at him to declare that he was a misfit, sometimes with physical blows. Like his siblings, he had been educated in the States as well as in France and elsewhere, while my grandfather was First Consul in Washington and greasing French oil supplies as Consul General in Texas. They wanted to be able to say their son was an Exonian – the American equivalent of an Etonian – but the fees were for people with industrial salaries rather than the diplomatic privileges my grand-parents enjoyed. To solve this, they got him to work in the school kitchen while he boarded there. The only time I ever sat with my uncle Mark in a car, he pulled the seat belt over his head as if he were donning an air mask, commentating quietly on his actions, then pawing the air with the catch unable to work out what to do next. The nickname Markie-too came from my mother's anxious questioning as a small child, 'And Markie too?', knowing that her brother would be excluded from the ice cream, the swimming party or the bike ride on offer.

On one of the rare stays when he was with us, my uncle Mark and I together took the implicit flak for not being 'joiners'. He and I seemed destined to be thrown together on that holiday, a satellite of the natural grouping. He was kind, eccentric and good at listening, and I was vaguely aware that I scrapped at his heels and elbows for atten-tion, and vaguely aware too of the ridicule I brought on myself in the eyes of some others in the family. Before we went on our trips to the Loire, I had no experience of riding a bicycle. The way I learned was probably one of the least calculated to make a skilful and confident cyclist. Markie-too was clearly as limited in his skill on two wheels as I was. Our method was to take the bicycle to the top of a small hill, where he recommended I get on the saddle and tip downwards. By force of gravity, the bicycle would move and I could declare myself a born cyclist. We did this again and again, never challenging flat ground to see if this worked in the same way. It was a good game that we shared, at least.

Driving to the gates of the property one morning on the way to get supplies from the village, we stopped as usual to open them. It was the task of the children to jump out and feed the metal tongue back from its groove and pull open gates with a screech and a clangour, pulling them back, but not as far as the high nettles clustering around the gateway. That day we held our breaths at the noise, not noise in the audible sense, but a message shouting in red paint, broken across the bars of the gates but raging its meaning at us. We saw red swastikas vivid on the old grey paint, spray-canned in the night and now pointing their scratchy arms at us. As we stood on the country lane in the middle of nowhere, suddenly people seemed to be watching us, hidden from view. Here, deep in remote countryside, perhaps the war had never ended, but lived on behind hedges and old farm buildings, and we would be hunted down, if not for our religion or our dark eyes then for our secret bad thoughts. It was probably the random outburst of extreme-right, jobless youngsters, bored after dark, far from the lights of towns and cities. It was nothing to do with us, only that we didn't belong there.

A convent of nuns kiving nearby was looking for bigger premises. My grandmother eventually negotiated a deal with them to take on the chateâu, leaving half of the land and the orangery for her chosen son. The nuns were anxious to move in before the winter, making repairs to the roof, lining the whole floor with linoleum and putting in lifts. In the distance, through the trees at the edge of the old swimming pool, I could see the rows of tall shuttered windows, concealing those interconnecting rooms. The sun leached the field and grey stonework of their detail and brightness, giving the scene the quality of an old Polaroid. It was my mother and I standing there, the randomness of it present in our minds, the alignment and misalignment of people and place that meant we were there, without my father and generally with only one of my mother's brothers in the accepted circle. Perhaps it would not continue like that for ever; perhaps the frailty of our own presence on that property pressed on us. We were ultimately guests after all, while another life ticked on in London.

Turning to my mother, I was half on the verge of saying something, something about a future dream dissolving as it came into contact with a well of nostalgia – something about our failed attempt to colonise the past – but she stopped me before I could formulate the thought. 'You mustn't regret,' she said with total firmness, these words spoken by a person who only occasionally allowed herself to give in to insomnia with an old game, furnishing in her head all the childhood rooms she had slept in, going back from Texas, to Ottawa, to Dublin, all the way back to Paris, and the room she and Markie-too had shared as tiny children.

It is nine at night the lowered gas burns you steal away
From the dormitory and all night in the college chapel
    pray
While everlastingly the flaming glory of Christ
Flames in adorable depths of amethyst
It is the fair lily that we all revere
It is the torch burning in the wind its auburn hair
It is the rosepale son of the mother of grief
It is the tree with the world's prayers ever in leaf
It is of honour and eternity the double beam
It is the six-branched star it is God
Who Friday dies and Sunday rises from the dead
It is Christ who better than airmen wings his flight
He holds the record of the world for height

Lines from 'Zone', in which Guillaume Apollinaire
remembered the school he went to in Monaco,
overlooking the Mediterranean while his mother worked
at the Royal Casino. It was run by an order of Marian
brothers, and it was there that he met René Dalize, 'the
oldest of all your friends', who was killed in action in
1917 and to whom he dedicated *Calligrammes*.

ENGLAND

Although our household was austere, bound by exacting rules of play, the formality of table manners, the expectation either of adult behaviour in children or a nineteenth-century level of discipline, this was fast going against the times. Yet when we were very little, 1979 and its winter of discontent was not far behind us. And not so far behind that was the legacy of privation handed on by the war. My mother and father were war babies – my mother did not even meet her father until she was three and he was on leave from China, where he spent the war as part of the French delegation to Chiang Kai-shek's government. I don't know how my paternal grandfather spent the war. My parents preceded the optimistic babyboomers. They were a little older than many of their friends with children the same age as us, and they had many older people among their friends. They had their feet more firmly planted in that receding age of austerity than in the growing prosperity of a boom generation. This marked my father's childhood, and his psyche. As he grew up, he was swept forward with the great age of social mobility and improvement that followed the war, and of the ideal then prevailing in England of an education that was selective but available to all. The grammar schools were elitist only in the sense that they pushed for the best, and I think that prompted his open embrace of elitism in its purely descriptive sense, with none of the apologetic notions that came to dog the idea later on.

He was proud of his education at Newcastle Royal Grammar. It was what pulled him up from a modest background, gave him the ambition to try for Oxford as a scholarship boy and go to London to work. His first job was back home on the railways. I can't imagine he would have been much good at sweeping the platforms, or at his next job as a waiter. He was probably a bit bored, though he would deny it in the name of eye-opening experiences, and he couldn't have balanced a loaded drinks tray very effectively. More than likely, he had a book in his pocket and took it out to read at every opportunity. But the job on the railway platforms was useful for the cut-price fares to London, he said, and he once served a drink to Vivien Leigh. She was playing at the Newcastle Playhouse and he still seemed to be reeling from setting eyes on her beauty close up. He dismissed talk of class – the English obsession – and sexism, because it was boring and counterproductive to dwell on them, and because he thought that society had finally evolved from them. In his eyes, people in general had the capacity to be free from those prejudices and outmoded inequalities. It was part of being civilised.

He was always looking for the signs of the future in the present, for the way things would go, the present seen as a provisional set of conditions. His thoughts were always moving from the detail to the big picture and back again, dismantling the monolithic view with his wit and denial of easy doctrine. Still, going up to Oxford in 1959 as a scholarship boy was the opening of a new world. The social contrast must have been startling, but without being one of the rowdy clubbable types, he threw himself in and thrived. Becoming a journalist was in some ways an extension of college life, a lot of clever people observing the world and writing it up in coruscating detail and with steely regularity. But Fleet Street and the newspaper world was also remarkable as an almost classless society, where what you said and wrote counted for everything, and where you came from counted for little. Competition came from another quarter, from the source of your own energies and application, from how quickly and sharply you responded to events, how much better you could do so than the other papers, and how well you could keep it up day after day, week after week.

The division between the two sides of my family set in early. My mother's side had no tolerance for my father or where he came from. My father rarely spoke about his childhood. As he was an only child, there were no other children to help bring us into contact with our northern roots, and because we packed off to France in all the holidays, we never got to know our paternal grandparents. It seemed – on a fundamental level – as though my father came from nowhere, a fully formed adult, a head on two shoulders, touching the sides of things and family only minimally. We did not even know his parents by name; they were simply called 'your English grandparents'. My English grandfather faded away when I was a young child. Years later, my mother told me his powers of speech and orientation had suddenly collapsed. Coming home from the doctor's one day, he sat down on the kitchen floor and said, 'I want to go home', then died the following day. My English grandmother survived alone in her two-up-two-down in Gateshead for several years, but apart from the occasional package in the post or a Christmas card with £5 tucked into it, we had no contact. My abiding image of my father's childhood was of a slight boy with a striking face trudging across the moors to school in short trousers. One of the few stories he told us from those days was that he and the other boys each owned only one jumper, but they had sent them to the orphans in Romania as part of a school charity appeal. So there he was, in short trousers and shirtsleeves, walking across the hills, blown by cold winds from the docks.

This image is probably a long way from the truth – or perhaps only a short way. I know this little boy spent a lot of time reading and thinking on his own, yet had a huge capacity for fun and excitement – for inspiration, above all. There lived in him a slightly dandyish quality, but you had to know him to see how layered and changeable his nature could be. It became a well-loved anecdote that he was turned down after one of the two interviews that led to his beginnings as a journalist because they considered him 'too frivolous'. He had the Wildean capacity to take light things seriously, and serious things lightly – and some of Wilde's maxims were old favourites, particularly 'If a thing is worth doing, it's worth doing badly'. But that's another way of saying life is to be taken seriously, and challenges risen to, and another way of expressing the comic fatalism of Beckett's words, 'Try again. Fail again. Fail better'. Life to my father was about the pursuit of excellence, but he loved the element of contradiction. He never voted in elections, because he said he always knew what the result was going to be, and not, as some journalists held, that it would compromise his impartiality as a commentator. That would have been to take himself far too seriously, although there was in a sense more superiority in the reason he gave, the effortless superiority perhaps credited to the people at Balliol, his Oxford college.

Except it was not effortless. Even with the gifts of an exceptional memory, unusual perceptiveness and the courage to be heterodox, being heavyweight came with a toll. I was very young when he started writing a book, a short and strongly argued case for European Union. The force field around this effort was powerful enough to create in me the assumption that writing a book was a place where only the mad dare go. Smoke billowed around his study door, I suppose only kept ajar for the necessary ventilation this provided, and because our house was full of malfunctioning fittings. That the door was not completely shut, though, added to the sense that this was a divide not to be mucked about with. The sound of the typewriter keys streamed into white noise, with a faster and more frequent ping of the carriage lever, bashed with the inner wrist as he hastened to the next line. He had elegant hands with pronounced veins. Over time they became more riven with tension, prone to sudden flicks or to his shaking them out to alleviate repetitive strain injuries. He had wanted to call his book *Can We Save this Marriage?* but his publishers opted for the more restrained as well as self-evident *Can We Save the Common Market?* In marriage as in markets, the answer to this question was a resounding yes, at least in spirit, but practice is more complicated.

In a decade dominated by colourful figures like Conrad Black, Jeffrey Archer and the Iron Lady herself, he wrote a wide-ranging weekly column in the *Financial Times* called 'Politics Today'. Despite his hard-headed ana lysis of the contemporary social and political landscape, always brought back to its economic base, he had little interest in material concerns at home, and dismissed them if they came up. Our house was haphazardly set up around these rifts. We were lucky to live in the centre of London, but the house itself was creaking at the seams. 'The wilds of Notting Hill', as some of my parents' friends knew it, preferring to move to sedate Hampstead when they got their first promotion, was not the same place in

1976 as it is now. The mansions of Ladbroke Grove had been built with a flaw: no mews houses to put the servants and carriages in. Whole streets had turned into slum housing, and the call for immigrants to work on the new public transport systems in the 50s brought an influx of poor families. The neglected old house my parents found scraped the right side of the north–south tracks of Kensington, and it was a long way from south of the river. It also stretched my parents' means from the word go. I realised later that my mother's parents had stepped in with an insistent offer to help them move from south to west London, but in a manner that had strings attached, even if these turned out to be very long.

My mother swapped her easel for a stepladder and painted and decorated it all herself, stitching and hanging curtains, and arranging the things she brought with her from her family. Of the two, she was definitely the one who was the more capable and prepared to get it done, not least for us children to live in. However many layers of wallpaper never concealed the frail plaster, the draughty windows and the chatter of loose floorboards that accompanied every other step. Radiators only ever seemed to be hot at the bottom, and no room was dedicated to relaxing in. Apart from around the dining or kitchen table, there was not one room we all spent time in together at the same time, except on Christmas Day or when my parents' friends came. It was less a matter of rigid rules than of an unspoken sense of this being the way things were, a balance not to be upset, a mood of tension not to be challenged. Yet there was less expectation of plushness and familiarity then. The house – by modern standards very uncomfortable – bore the marks of an older aesthetic, with old paintings, Chinese ginger jars and the drawing-room doors to the garden hanging with green-gold silk brocade from Les Vallières. The curtains were made for much higher windows, even higher than the ones in that room, and always hung unhemmed in a great pile on the floor, in deference to the heavy old weave and its intricate trimmings.

Our weekends revolved around the park, the library and church on Sundays. On Saturday mornings, we shuttled around Notting Hill and Portobello on errands, bouncing on the back seat with no concern for seat belts. Hurtling down Ladbroke Grove, we called out optimistically, 'It's the steepest hill in the wooorld!' We were a little more orderly if my father was in the car, in case he was in a particularly serious mood and in case my mother was angry because she'd had to ferry him as well as us around again. If he was with us, it was because we were dropping him off by the prison at Wormwood Scrubs for his weekly game of tennis. We sniggered as we watched him and his friend Norman Lamont, striding off with grave sporting purpose to find their court. Their identical tennis whites accentuated the contrast between their heights and girths – like Little and Large, we used to say, pleased to be able to make a reference from television, and one comprehensible to other people.

On Saturday afternoons, my mother often took us to Kensington Library and left us there while she caught up on whatever she needed to do. This might have been going down the other side of the hill to Portobello Market, where she took a stall and sold paintings and bric-a-brac. She could pull on stores of knowledge about Sèvres, Ming, cloisonné enamel, varieties of jade, solid silver over EPNS, oil as opposed to gouache, engravings as distinct from prints. She had an eye for it that came in useful for selling and dealing. Meanwhile, we had fun at the library – like the park and the church, it was both free and safe. I loved that building, vast, hushed and imbued with purpose. My sisters and I stayed there for hours, until the particular clack-clack of my mother's heels on the floor made me lift my head from the pages over which I was curled in the window seat.

If my mother didn't drop us off at the local library, she told my father he had to take us to the park, a reluctant ritual at first but as good as my mother's promise, we all loved it when we got there. The best thing about our house was where it was; the way it was so close to two parks, Hyde Park and Kensington Gardens on one side, and Holland Park on the other, each offering distinct delights. Holland Park was smaller but filled with greater variety, with paths that were surprisingly thickly wooded, the intricately designed Flower Garden and the rough-and-tumble adventure playground, which I mainly remember for the tree logs horizontally placed on two forked stumps at its entrance. If you were small enough to go under it, you were not allowed in, and that seemed to go on for an unfairly long time in my case. Peacocks, rabbits and squirrels were rampant in this park. My mother used to tell the story of the girl who was transformed into a peacock for falling in love with the wrong boy. She had her heart set on a boy named Leon, and trapped in her peacock body spent the rest of her life calling for him, 'Le-on! Le-on!' On quiet nights, we could sometimes hear the peacock's cry from our own garden, the throaty garble 'Leon!' sounding its mournful air. If you know the sound of a peacock's cry, you'll know it is her calling the boy's name.

Hyde Park was a bigger expedition, the playground representing almost a mythical distance to be charted, the sunken garden beyond it and the Peter Pan tree in the league of a seldom-attained fantasy. We sometimes took along the 'I Heart New York' Frisbee my father had brought back from New York to our great excitement. None of us showed much prowess with it, though, and games were probably dampened too by the endless squabbling of three girls very close in age, not least my whining at being condemned to be piggy-in-the-middle again to sustain the bigger ones' games of catch. Tug-of-war was a game my father seemed to know of old, but his limited attempts at bringing out my sporting side had even more limited success. He sometimes claimed I might be becoming a 'bluestocking'. Despite the joking tone, it was apparent as much as it was confusing to me that he was making a point. Once I realised what it meant, I wondered what sort of stocking he expected me to be, given the knit of his own mind.

The Round Pond was more accessible, perhaps because my father liked it most of all. Its surface always moving, glinting or breathing mist, it acted as a natural magnet, drawing families to its orbit where flocks of birds ebbed. Often a lone eccentric set up a box of equipment by a bench and spent the morning free-sailing model boats across it. Even then it was a place where I almost felt I could catch the unchangeable fleetingly in my hand. The past seemed to connect with the present and future, our age differences levelled by the ritual of feeding the birds, in a kind of trance induced by the honk of geese, the tameness of ducks reliably hungry for old bread, the weird muscular strains in the swans' necks and their striking whiteness even in the dullest weather. London has little of the classical beauty of Paris, but that scene is an exception and I wished my mother would accompany us when we went there too, instead of farming us out to my father alone for a blast of fresh air at the weekends.

Near the park and the entrance to the church where my mother took us on Sunday mornings, an old tramp lived on the bench. Like the rag-and-bone man who came by our house on his cart making his incomprehensible cry, the tramp seemed to me to hark back to past times. Nothing like modern colours or materials touched his vague outline. He was covered in rags, bearded and filthy. But it felt like something that he lived on the bench, and for such a long time that it was indisputably his home. He was a fixture of the neighbourhood and he stayed there with his plastic bags stuffed with more rags and old newspapers until he died. I don't think I was the only one who felt sad then, for his disappearance and perhaps too for the disappearance of a tolerance of the poor and shambolic mixed in with the yuppies instead of pushed from view as if they no longer existed.

My father never came to church with us. He was not militant in the way he expressed it or sneering to those who were of different persuasions, but he was not at all religious. Nor was he agnostic; he thought religion was the single greatest pretext for war in history. He saw churches in only an artistic, architectural and historical light. To my mother it was part of the fabric of things, and her hour there 'with my three girls' was the only moment of the week when she claimed she felt 'completely at peace'. By this point in the day, she would already have peeled another small mountain of potatoes, made an apple tart and put the roast in the oven, the roast that offset the leek and potato soup and cheese we ate the rest of the weekend.

❧

My mother had never lived in London before arriving there with her English husband and growing family. My grandmother had been so affronted by their making their first home in Clapham – 'of all places!' – that she had arranged for a sum of money to be made over to them to buy a house in a better neighbourhood. The difficult circumstances of my parents buying the house in Notting Hill with their toddler speaking her first few words in a mixture of languages and another small baby were further complicated by the fact that my mother was on the brink of giving birth to me. She was away in Denmark in the maternity ward, where my father had no intention of joining her, and the logistics of the house were left to be worked out remotely between him and my grandmother. Looking back, it seems they never recovered a sense of civility towards each other after whatever passed in this dialogue.

My grandmother's parents had had their country house in Clapham before the Victorian housing boom, but the world had moved on and so had she, and she had no sentimental attachments to the place. We had one photograph, a tiny image of a carriage and a footman in a top hat and tails drawing up outside a large front door, my great-grandparents ready to alight at their home. Now Clapham was one of the scruffy suburban districts of London, far from diplomatic quarters and far from Knightsbridge, where my grandmother had quietly kept a flat all of her own during my mother's childhood. Years later, my mother pointed out the flat behind Harrods where her mother used to meet a lover whether her husband was away with the French embassy or not. It is startling that my grandmother was able to exert so much influence on how we set ourselves up, but my parents had very little money of their own so they capitulated to moving to a bigger house in an up-and-coming neighbourhood, innocent of the fact that when it came to my grandmother, help was never as simple as that.

My sisters, particularly the older one, had known the house in Clapham slightly. It had a similar layout to the one in Notting Hill, with steps running either up or down to a long garden. There is a photograph of Emma with her squared fringe and her kilt held up by wide straps of tartan over the shoulders. Another little girl is in the picture too, a girl on a tricycle. She has the long floppy hair we were never allowed to have, because '*les petites filles bien élevées*' didn't have long hair. My father, in one of the tight nylon polo necks he used to wear on weekends with a blazer, is leaning behind her and motioning her onwards down the garden path. His arms are open wide in an unfamiliar paternal gesture. The girl is little, but bigger than us, definitely born before we were. This photograph was my only glimpse of the house in Clapham. The little girl with the long floppy hair and the tricycle disappeared with the house.

The question of whether this money for the house was a loan or a gift from my grandparents was never resolved. My parents couldn't afford to pay it back, in the same way that they could barely afford to keep up the house we lived in. Our existence there rested precariously on unspoken agreements. It also seemed safe to ignore how things had come about, and to carry on extending the mortgage in order to roll it into school fees. As my mother has a sense of style, and for the two of them other priorities prevailed, the house and our family of five had a certain symmetry to it, somehow frayed but lasting.

We were entering the loadsamoney decade and a time of relaxation of the old traditions. The 80s had London in their greedy grip. But this felt, from my earliest memories, like a bright bonfire always just beyond our reach. This was clear from my earliest memories. In the queue for the classroom after the register was taken in the children's playground, one little boy kept on pointing at the sky saying, 'ET phone home' in a funny voice. We were all of five years old and a discussion was rippling down the line of coloured macs and duffle coats. As I tried to wriggle out the mitten that was stuck somewhere in the armpit of my coat, and equalise it with the other one that trailed on a hopelessly long string of wool, I registered what they were talking about. It was the first time I remember noticing the impact of our not having one of the new-on-the-market Betamax players that delivered the world of *ET* and *Back to the Future* to family sitting rooms. These were swiftly superseded by the VHS, and so began the cycle of new models chasing the dying sheen of the older ones. The often desperate desire of children to be the same as their peers, exemplified in having the same things, was so far from the conversation in our house that we quickly swallowed the implicit message that it was all right to be eccentric.

In any case, it was still relatively early days for home entertainment. My father took this objective view, pointing out that far from all households in Britain had a video player – most didn't. It was a subtle projection – but there nonetheless – that his own children might be acting like the complacent 'haves' in our desire to have more and better television and video in our lives. There might be more to learn from remaining part of the majority 'have-nots' in this regard, was the suggestion. We could wait and see where television would take us. Let's not forget the medium is in its infancy. At Christmas, when our minds were on the films and shows that other families would be watching, his mind was elsewhere again, on the piece he had to write. *Financial Times* readers would be expecting to sit down with a long and considered article on the state of play not long after Boxing Day when the tinsel had settled.

One year my father was thinking that he might write a lighter, more seasonal kind of piece. He thought he'd make the case for Shakespeare as the greatest person who ever lived, when friends and colleagues suggested to him that the paper might instead run a competition for readers to put in their own nominations. This was the question he brought to the dinner table. We turned over the case for and against Jesus, Einstein and Shakespeare, and were all surprised when he put the piece together that Disney got a passionate vote. Funnier was Joe Bloggs, who got a vote for reliably putting up with it all, and Murphy for being responsible for so much in his infamous law yet continuing to be so elusive. Here my father seemed not at all out of step with the English sense of humour, its eccentricity and sympathy for the underdog.

The party conference season in October always took him off to Brighton or Blackpool, the beachside resorts exuding a rundown quality my father condemned as 'decadence' in one of his many impassioned perceptions of the everyday. At one of our parties, a female colleague of his gave me a snapshot of what it was like at the conferences with friends and workmates, once released from the packed halls and brightly lit stages of the political debates. Under the dark October sky, they went down to the beach and she tried to keep up with my father running along the shingle, hurling speeches from *Hamlet* and *Macbeth* over the black roar of the sea – 'To die, to sleep, To sleep, perchance to dream! Ay, there's the rub.' The short line was the one my sisters and I always remembered, with its faintly comic poise before the philosophical magnitude of our 'mortal coil'.

The year after the Brighton bombing, in the mid-80s, the world seemed constantly rocked by one crisis or another, with the unions raging and calling for strikes. Amazonian women with razor-sharp cheekbones smeared with sparkly reds, and even sharper shoulder pads stalked the catwalks. Getting in the car for school I asked my mother, 'Mummy, can a man be the prime minister?' Mrs Thatcher was the one who had survived the bombing by an extraordinary chance, as she went next door to the bathroom in the middle of the night while working characteristically late. She concluded afterwards in her resonant voice, 'The conference must go on!' We hardly needed a more formidable male role model. Whatever you thought of her, and I knew we were physically far away from the picket lines and steel factories, she was outstanding for at least one fact: that she was a woman. Those closest to her either loved or loathed her, so the gossip went, but those far from her also tended to condemn or adore her hands down. In our house, she seemed to be viewed with a constantly shifting critical eye; sometimes she was good, sometimes she was bad, but even with the ample good luck and lack of opposition she enjoyed, it was not patronising to state that one of her most remarkable achievements was that she was a woman leader in opposition and in power.

In our house, the news was woven into the furniture, newsprint leaving its grubby traces over seats and cushions. Preparing for one of their dinner parties, my father once asked my mother to buy some toy helicopters for their friend Leon Brittan. It was his birthday and though my parents never went in for presents much, the helicopters were really a joke. It was Leon Brittan, then Trade and Industry Secretary, who stood by Mrs Thatcher in the bid for the ailing Westland helicopters to merge with an American rather than a European company, a complicated scandal that saw Michael Heseltine and his outrageous hair march straight out of the cabinet. The Westland Affair seemed a small business to me and too technical to get a firm grip on, but it was the big news story for ages, nearly bringing the government down and spoken of for years afterwards. I remember admiring the shiny primary colours on the helicopters' boxes as they were wrapped up in grown-up wrapping paper and given away to a grown man as part of a baffling joke.

We were walking to Notting Hill Gate one day, the wind picking up as usual on the wide crossroads. I had a win in my pocket – 120 francs won on the Lotto – and my father was taking me to the post office to open an account with it. It was a notable win, as we only ever bet a few francs as one of our holiday rituals in France. I felt lucky as I tried to match his adult strides, the skirt of his raincoat flapping at my knees behind him, even though I was slightly embarrassed to bring back the spoils of my summer holidays. His mind was on other things: would the Post Office be privatised, and would we have so many of them

My father at a party conference

in future? He started to expand on the idea of developing technology. For example when better computers were invented, and there were scanners instead of ticket collectors, and automated response systems instead of people on the telephone, then work would no longer exist in the same way. We could be looking at a society that no longer could or should seek a full working week from most people. Unemployment was one of the biggest problems of the decade; I knew that from him and also that Mrs Thatcher overlooked it again and again, but there might be a way of looking at the problem more creatively. He certainly didn't work an ordinary week – other fathers went to work in the morning and came back in the evening; many parents I knew did this after sitting down for a communal breakfast. Work could mean inventing new things, he was saying, and we could spend more time reading and thinking. I wondered if my 120 francs had anything to do with this. It was radical advice, and made me think, though what practical action it required was trickier to pin down or to connect with my winning piece of paper.

❧

One of the bookshelves at home was lined with my father's Everyman library of poetry books, each a small hardback with the dust jacket in a different colour. For no particular reason, he might take one out and give it to me with nondescript words like 'Here, read this'. There in pale blue, I found Emily Dickinson, a woman who stood out in her time for refusing marriage, and instead writing poems about what she felt and things she had never seen, punctuating them only with dashes, like the breaths I imagined her taking from her pillowed corner in the bedroom where she spent most of her time, or like the stitches with which she sewed her poems together in bundled paper packages. In a yellow leaf colour, I found Gerard Manley Hopkins, the Catholic convert priest who developed a unique and exuberant metrical system based on medieval sources, and whose quiet solitude 'on a pastoral forehead of Wales' obscured the duelling seasons of his inner life, between the blazing tempest of his relationship with God and the dappled sunshine of the physical world that awed him with joy and beauty. My father was transported by their stories and their words, and I wondered what struggle or what susceptibility might have led him to that.

His advice on reading books differed radically from my grandfather's. Not only was reading every word on every page assumed as the starting point, but if he had one of the Arden Shakespeares open on his lap, he tapped lightly on the footnotes as a reminder to read each one. Then you could learn something about the different ways Shakespeare can be interpreted. 'Always try to read more than one work by the same author,' was another counsel. 'And you might make it a lesser-known one.' He didn't have much time for novels, other than the many thin Penguins on the shelf – mainly by Graham Greene, Anthony Powell and Evelyn Waugh – because they were so long and 'so few of them are any good'. I think this was another way of saying that no other form gives the same emotional intensity as poetry.

❧

Theatre was my father's passion, of all the arts, and something he had loved since his Oxford days – and Shakespeare was his favourite playwright for the simple reason that he combined being a poet and a dramatist with greater scope than anyone else. As children, my father took us to see *West Side Story*, a good musical even allowed for none of the chopping and changing of today's writing. He composed his pieces from end to end in one.

Of all the plays we went to see together, I found *Waiting for Godot* the most astounding – something must have prepared me for it being desperate and funny in equal measure. It was extraordinary to find out that Beckett, an Irishman, had first written *Waiting for Godot* in French. In addition to his plays, and my mother's American edition of Beckett's trilogy of novels, my father showed me his poems. Besides his own, not at all funny poems, Beckett had also translated some of the best modern French poetry. Flicking through the pages, I found a long poem called 'Zone' by Apollinaire, the same poet who had written what I had taken for a children's rhyme about the cat that my grandfather and I knew by heart. It came from the same collection as 'Le Pont Mirabeau', a mysteriously sad love poem I had learned at school, evoking the Seine running for ever under the bridge in Paris – with the repeated refrain 'The days go by, I remain'. I'd often looked at the photograph of the Pont Mirabeau in the Apollinaire book I had found in my father's study. This poem now took its place in my mind as the lullaby that accompanied the picture. In the book, it was called his poem of '*fin d'amour*', because relations with his lover Marie were floundering, although it's impossible to read that story into the words. Only the feeling is there. If I didn't know the intricacies of the poet's story then, in the lines of the poetry was something I understood.

on the old divan in his apartment, stuffed with books and curiosities picked up from flea markets and stalls along the banks of the Seine. Here in 'Zone' was the Paris blueprint.

I went back to the bilingual book about this mysterious poet I had found among my father's books and papers. A cartoonish sketch by Picasso adorns the front; the poet, is hook-nosed and pensive, smoking his pipe. Bound into the book's spine is a yellow ribbon, and a few pages in a clear plastic sleeve, the sort you might find in an old-fashioned photo album. Inside the sleeve is another drawing by Picasso, Apollinaire's friend from their earliest beginnings as poor artistically minded migrants. I teased out the picture, hoping its protective cover would not turn out to be too brittle but it seemed as good as new. The sketch – done on *papiers à carreaux*, the squared paper found in school exercise books and *papeteries* all over France and that my grandfather wrote in – fitted in the palm of my hand. Picasso has done his friend up in the guise of a matador, smoking a pipe again, but in elaborate costume with cape and cravat, with the words Don Guillermo Apollinaire at the top in the artist's messy handwriting. They had landed in Paris around the same time, Picasso from Malaga and Apollinaire from the Côte d'Azur, as the twentieth century opened. Picasso pictured his friend as the don of the bullfight, the Spanish national pastime that was in the artist's blood. The token of friendship was a profound act of love and respect, a linking of hands across culture and *métier*. I read 'Zone' and 'Le Pont Mirabeau' repeatedly, reciting them to myself, and started to match the pieces of the poet's story with what he called his poems of '*fin d'amour*'. In different ways, my father and my grandfather had drawn me to these poems and they started to become a receptacle for all the elusive qualities they embodied.

Now you walk in Paris alone among the crowd
Herds of bellowing buses hemming you about
Love's anguish sears you from within
As if you would never be loved again
If you lived in ancient times you could get you to a
  cloister
You are ashamed when you catch yourself at a
paternoster
You mock yourself and like hellfire your laughter
cackles
Golden on your life's hearth fall the sparks of your
  laughter
It is a painting hung in a sombre museum
And sometimes you go and look at it up close

Lines from 'Zone' as the poet remembers the ones
he loved and lost.

BEFORE YOU WERE BORN

I never saw any photographs of my parents' wedding day, or knew anything about it, so it was a surprise to me when my mother dropped a few fragments in passing about how they met. They walked into each other's lives by chance in Paris. She had returned there as a young woman, a still naïve Ivy League graduate who had gravitated first to New York. She was neither Americanised enough nor Parisian any more, and was washed up by the American dream – though she always maintained she came back to Paris on the back of an unaffordable dentist's bill. When she got back to the country of a childhood more distant in place and culture than in time, she was alone as her parents had gone off to live in Africa and her brothers were still in school. She was almost a stranger to Paris. So was my father. He was there on assignment from the paper in London.

My mother moved into an apartment in the 16th arrondissement which my grandparents had recently rented, as was the custom. It was newly decorated according to my grandmother's design, and it remained the same for another forty years and for all the time I knew it. Paris is small but much more densely populated than London, the dream of an efficient modern city of apartment blocks now a bygone *belle époque*. But for all the tall apartment buildings lining the narrow streets with hundreds of residences, there were very few people outside, at least in that area. Everyone seemed to live behind shutters or be at work or away, and their cars were kept in underground garages. Down from the Étoile and near the borderland of fast cars before the city opens out to the Bois de Boulogne, my grandparents' building stood in a typical sombre uniform row. The back of the building looked into a well, the typical sunless inner space where rubbish was kept, and which separated the larger front of the block from the back where the servants' rooms were meant to be. As there was little view at the front, apart from other windows similarly obscured by curtains and shutters, so there is even less at the back. Starved of natural light, my grandmother brought shades of colour into the apartment by hanging textured materials on the walls.

Every inch of the interior was covered in something soft and dark, brocade or velvet stripes or a seagrass weave. The kitchen was connected to the rest of the apartment by a long corridor, lined with this dried grass stuff and divided into two by a blue curtain loosely tied at its waist like a voluminous ball gown. The layout dated from times when guests were kept away from the bustle and smell of cooking, and servants would bring covered dishes all the way down the corridor to the dining room. Bedrooms

and bathrooms were off the corridor, turned on the inter
ior of the building with no view. The walls and sealed
windows made the whole place feel like a velvet vacuum,
caught in the past like Paris itself through depressed eyes.
My mother was being sucked into the velvet-padded past,
made a stand-in mother to her younger brothers while
her parents were in Africa, leading a life that wasn't hers
any more. Then she met my father.

It was May 1968, and the bar of the Crillon Hotel was
heaving. My mother was working as a translator for the
United Nations, and my father was a young reporter.
Hundreds of international delegates were gathering in
Paris for the Vietnam Peace Talks, a desperate call for
American withdrawal from Vietnam that came as the Tet
Offensive raged through Saigon and US ground troops
massacred the villages. Far from this bloodshed, looking
out on the man-made plain of the Place de la Concorde,
the neoclassical façade of the Crillon was ablaze with
artificial light. Inside, the bar hummed like a subterranean city blowing chimneys of smoke above its inhabit-
ants' heads, in defiance of the celestial glories depicted
above. From a grand piano, the chords of a Chopin tune
competed with the shouts of conversation in several
languages. The building was then owned by the Taittinger
family, and ever since then and the quantities they drank

in the Crillon bar, it has been my mother's favourite champagne. She was talking to a very tall, charming, blue-eyed young journalist named Peter Snow. All of a sudden he said, 'Oh look, here comes Juliet.' It was my father coming towards them, an old college friend of Snow's, it turned out, the one who sometimes took the women's parts in plays because he looked so much better in a dress than his friends. He played a particularly memorable Juliet. That was the beginning of their 'Romeo and Juliet' love story.

They arranged to meet as soon as possible the following day, when my father would begin gathering what he needed for his article on the prospects for peace in Vietnam, while unexpectedly trying to impress his new friend. My mother was keen to help the up-and-coming journalist find his way around Paris. The script was changing around them. It was no longer a delegation of ideas-men trying to seize the day to stop war: the students in the suburbs were rallying; the young were on the streets. In the morning, the Boulevard Saint-Germain bore the scars of the night before, burnt-out cars and broken placards blowing in the gutter. The heart of Paris was filling with student protestors again, heading towards the Sorbonne where police stood guard outside the quarantined headquarters inside which a few beleaguered administrators and professors sweated. Black spraypaint graffitied metal shop shutters with the paradoxes of a new generation – they had cars but they wanted freedom; they had televisions but they wanted their imaginations to run wild; they had comfort but they rejected boredom, hierarchy, consumerism. Student ideals played imperfectly but violently into the demands of factory workers and union members, tipping street demonstrations into hand-to-hand fighting, into a national crisis of strike action, riot policing and political survival.

Hand in hand on the rippling edge of the crowd, my parents adventured with them, the ricochet of slogans telling them a parallel private story, weaving itself beneath the opportunism of new news. 'Take your desires for reality', 'Make Love Not War,' came the instructions from shouts and banners. Could they make an alternative to *métro-boulot-dodo* living? Neither of them knew the habits the other had already acquired, the promises they might already have made. In Paris, the young had noticed that the creeping habits of the commute-work-commute way of life could be resisted, had to be, as there was another way to be. 'I'm a Groucho Marxist' and other spoofs on the old war cries made a joke of taking politics too seriously, and a dare to take youth and freedom more seriously. Only those who lacked imagination failed to imagine what was lacking. Elliptical palindromes, written with the ephemeral brashness of youth, pushed an anarchic message – amusing, heartfelt, sinister and probably doomed to fail. 'The walls have ears, your ears have walls,' they said, and television gave this a new slant too. It was the first mass demonstration and civil battle to be so heavily filmed, gaining scale and momentum from the lenses trained on it and the screens rolling it out.

A fierce stinging to the eyes, like the effect of chopping a pile of onions, told my parents it was getting more serious. Close to the Sorbonne, robot men with truncheons set off white clouds of tear gas. Siren calls drowned out the shouting for a moment, but it was not stopping. They pushed through to where the crowds were thinning at the fringes of the Latin Quarter, pressing on to the river, away from the Left Bank. Beyond, my mother had a friend with a telephone, which my father desperately needed in order to contact the paper in London.

Lone men ran through the middle of streets, kicking up cobbles and calling, '*Sous les pavés, la plage!*', 'Poetry is in the streets' and 'Life is in the streets'. A maniacal energy threw young left-wing intellectuals into identifying with every struggle – 'We are all untouchables', 'We are all German Jews', 'How can we think freely in the shadow of the Church?' Women in short loud-patterned skirts and black polo necks screamed and kissed. More police manned the entrances to the bridges. They accosted my parents as they tried to cross, not letting anyone leave the area without a confrontation. Further along the Seine, a cool spring breeze swaying the plane trees made a sound like the sea, and blooms of narcissi were visible on the wide pavement. They headed towards the Pont Mirabeau, the last of the central Paris bridges, leading over to the village district of Auteuil. Exhilarated by their flight through Paris in the blaze of riots, in the spring, absorbing all the urgency of my father's press deadline, my mother unleashed her fury on the policeman attempting to hold them up on the bridge. Using every strategy she had, including heavy name-dropping and threats to report him to the Ministry where her father was a doyen, she finally slapped the policeman's face and they carried on. In the middle of the Pont Mirabeau, the raging sounds of street battles subsided, mixing to an indistinct rumble behind the call of gulls over the water. The view of Paris settled like a painting, its skyline a collision of classical with modern now mutely describing the seething tensions of May's events.

I always remember that apartment in the 16th arrondissement for its mixture of both beauty and entrapment. The entrance hall was a square room entirely lined in dark-red brocade, a gilt mirror exaggerating its effects. The other object hanging on the wall was a portrait of a curly-wigged, ruff-necked fellow painted in a nacreous layer over a convex surface, so that nothing in this space seemed straightforwardly tactile. All windows hung with gauze, tinged slightly grey, as well as heavy curtains. It was a shock when I lifted the heavy red curtains over the front door to find a clunking metal fire door and lock behind it, making an indestructible barrier between it and the original bevelled wood of the exterior front door. In this way, the sound of neighbours inside and out was muffled for us, and they were never seen either. We spent concertinaed

Christmas holidays there, piling into the dark childless interconnecting rooms to stay with my grandparents.

My middle sister and I slept on those camp beds made of a layer of canvas stretched over a metal frame. Milla and I thought these beds, which looked and felt more like army stretchers, were pretty funny for being typical of my grandfather's boot camp approach. In the mornings, we were to fold up our sheets and hang the stretchers from hooks at the kitchen end of the corridor. I think my older sister shared one of the sofa beds with my mother. It was lucky that my father didn't accompany us, in a way. I wondered both at my parents' not spending more time together and at the awkward arrangements in France, but the balance of power was such in my grandparents' domain that my mother was perpetually the sole daughter, whose children would squeeze in along with her.

My grandfather was now fully confined to his room, and in Paris there was a monolithic divide between inside and outside. He often wore his navy-blue dressing gown and leather slippers all day, going only from bed to chair. His oxygen machine stood next to the trolley where my grandmother placed his lunch and dinner, and his essentials were within reach. He had pills, inhalers, Badoit, a pot of Dijon mustard, a pot in which to put his teeth, pens and notebook, a radio, a jar of cheese crackers to eat before dinner and packets of Petit Beurre biscuits for in between. The two of us were still sometimes left at home together, so that he didn't get too lonely. It became more like a summons into the shadows, I felt guiltily. I was less at ease babbling in French and making up stories spontaneously. His laboured breathing seemed to carry the burden of a great sadness, though maybe only the sadness of no longer being young and healthy rather than for anything we had done. We sometimes resorted to sitting in silence, or he might stroke my hair once saying, '*Elle a bonne mine.*' It sounded like a mixture of regret and amazement that I had the glow of life in my cheeks.

The city was an incidental backdrop to my grandmother's errands. We held on tight in the back of her old Renault, her personal downtime car, as she hurtled along, dodging bumper cars that never bumped despite the lane-free madness around the Champs Elysées. She kept up a tongue-twisting trail of gossip about the goings-on at her club, the *Cercle Interallié*. The city was like a beautiful accident that had arrived, unlike London, in a fully formed master plan. Its vistas are surface-deep, either too far or too near for the re-enactment of love stories. Paris too is a dream that can't be reached.

My mother's version of Paris sees its beauty only through the lens of melancholy, only as a window on the past and the unattainable, and as a forgotten bridge between her past and her future with my father. She was very unhappy when she went back there, a stranger in her first home, no longer part of the American way her parents had thrown her into as a child. My grandfather held an ideal – formed by the war – of a future in the States and a special relationship with it. Lodging her with an elderly couple when they left Texas for Washington, where she drove herself to her prom dance while her brothers were scattered in boarding schools, didn't help to make an American of my mother. Her parents exerted their power over thousands of miles, expecting her to look after her younger brothers when they came back from school and 'keep up' the apartment in unfeasibly complicated ways, with multiple secret bank accounts, hiding places for keys and security codes, and people whom Madame Robert needed to keep in the grip of her needs. Meeting my father turned her head. She did not know what she was in for, but she wanted to go with him. Within a year they were married and starting a new life, not in Paris or London but in Germany.

Under the Pont Mirabeau
Runs the Seine
And our loves
Must I be reminded again
Love comes always after pain
Come night the hour strikes
The days go by and I remain

Poem written by Apollinaire inspired by his lover, the painter Marie Laurencin, and the bridge he crossed to go home to his apartment in Auteuil.

☙

Bonn is 'a small town in Germany' – the title of John le Carré's novel nails in an understatement its mixture of a backwater quality and its seat at the heart of Europe's struggles two decades on from the war. It was either the weather or the trains, went the running joke of everyone's existence there. Plain functional structures were interspersed with clumps of nineteenth-century buildings running with dark beams in Germanic style. In the 70s, Europe was mired in post-war politics and deeply divided between East and West. In this still bucolic setting, a recently made capital that would be unmade again before long, my father was gaining his first big break in journalism. The *Financial Times* offered him the job of Chief Correspondent in West Germany in 1969 and he took it. Though my parents had only just met, they married and packed off to a divided Germany, where they lived for four years, and where my older sister was born.

In a place without history, my parents set up their first home. They threw themselves into it with all the optimism of the first uphill ride – although my mother disliked the German language and feared the people. My mother did all the driving, and every time they went to Berlin or beyond, sat gripping the steering wheel and staring straight ahead as officers searched the boot before they could cross Checkpoint Charlie, dividing West from East. The only time my father ever invoked a name for personal advancement was when he and my pregnant mother were interrogated crossing the border from Romania back to the West. 'Name?' 'Rutherford.' 'Are you related to Lord Rutherford, the great physicist who split the atom?' 'Yes!' my father answered. Knowing how potent rank and scientific achievement were for opening doors in communist countries, this ruse was the only way to get across the border. He could be relatively certain that the guards would not know Rutherford was a run-of-the-mill name in northeastern England, and this particular Rutherford had only the skimpiest of scientific ability.

In anticipation of her first child's birth, my mother frantically called the local authorities. For some reason, she suspected the baby might be a boy. A boy born in Germany of French-English parents rang alarm bells in her mind. She needed to know what kind of passport he would have. She could not stand the idea that her child might be compelled to do his military service in the German army.

But my father loved Germany, and they went together to every political and cultural party and event, meeting everybody, my father filing a piece, if not more, every day. He learned German quickly, gaining much more confidence in it than he ever would in French, not surprisingly, given his lack of relationship with his in-laws. After he returned to work at the *Financial Times* in London, his European outlook expanded the paper's coverage. Seeing British patterns and habits as relative to those of other nations, particularly those of what he saw as their natural allies, the French and the Germans, influenced his political views and his writing. It was backed up by history and experience, living in a city created over the top of the detritus of war, and in a country blighted by a divide. Perhaps it was drawn too from the absence of a father during the war. This was true for both my parents' first years and – even if it turned out they had little to do with each other – my father knew his father-in-law had led his career far from the safety of Paris, and spent the war on De Gaulle's mission to Chungking. This European, and international outlook set my father apart from many of his fellows.

Four years on, and it was time to do a different job, as well as to bring a daughter home. My parents gave their leaving party in the Bahnhof Rolandseck, a vast nineteenth-century train station that doubled as a ballroom, decked out with chandeliers, brocades and balustrades. At the party, attended by journalists, diplomats, writers and academics, the curator of this cultural centre and the party's host presented my parents with a book he had published and was particularly proud of. It wears the classic white livery of Gallimard editions – a small hardback with a fat leather spine. Neat lines gold-tooled across it frame the title, *Guillaume Apollinaire*. Apollinaire, who went on to become one of the first great modernists, had been a local; he had lived in a house near Bonn, and gone on a journey through Germany and eastwards to Vienna and Prague. He left a piece of himself behind, and continued all his life to correspond with German magazines, writers, artists and galleries. The book opens with a poem called 'Rolandseck', reflecting the poet's time on the edge of the Rhine, and the life of a European observer.

The book came straight from the part of my parents' lives that was the furthest away from mine, in the hidden circumstances of their first meeting and their early marriage. It was only later – after my grandfather's and my father's deaths – that I began obsessively to seek out the poems Apollinaire had written, as my family's roots drifted apart, though for a long time this compulsion pulled me along without conscious reason. I pieced together the poet's story, a displacement activity that gradually took me back to my own family's past and the places we had been. Apollinaire had spent his childhood on the Mediterranean, where his mother secretly drew financial support from his absent father's aristocratic relatives. He was poor and on his own, while the image

My parents in Bonn

of his ancestors' grandeur loomed over his mother and a past he barely experienced. To him, those roots were almost effaced by both his parents walking away from the long-established families they came from. Paris was the place for poets and writers, and was supposed to bring him work, but he gladly took the money and the prospects for travel that his tutoring job in Germany offered. My parents' apartment in Bonn, where my older sister was born, was a few miles from the chateâu of 'Neu-Glück', New Happiness, belonging to the pseudo-countess whose daughter's lessons Apollinaire was in charge of. They overlooked the same green misty hills, and they felt the same leaf-scented or squally winds from the nearby river.

This half-hidden book belonging to my parents, uncovered by me, celebrated the part of Apollinaire's life I had not imagined was anything other than disconnected from mine. In Germany, he fell in love for the first time, with the English governess who looked after the girl he tutored. Twice, love drove him all the way to London in pursuit of the English rose he had fallen for – to Clapham where she and her family lived. There he was, the poet, stalking my past again. When I came across the Apollinaire book, obscured by reams of paper in my father's study, its contents were half forgotten, a canvas to be rediscovered by me. To my parents it was only a curious memento from their time way back in Bonn when they were first married, an object with fragments of a story to tell that had been long overlaid with other stories.

My glass is filled with a wine that trembles like a flame
Listen to the slow song of the boatman
Who tells of having seen beneath the moon seven
  women
Shaking out their hair long and green to their feet

The Rhine the Rhine is drunk where the vines are
  mirrored
All the nights' gold falls trembling in their reflection
The voice sings again a song of mourning
These green-haired fairies who enchant the summer
My glass shatters like a burst of laughter

One of the sonnets set in the Rhineland, drafted in 1903 when Apollinaire lived there acting as a tutor to a young girl, and where he fell in love with the English governess Annie Playden. It was published in final form in his 1913 collection *Alcools*.

stationed outside in case anyone was threatened – really a precaution taken because members of the Cabinet were attending. Outside the house one year, my father was standing in his smartest suit in front of a man with a microphone and another man with a camera. The man started to speak: 'What do you think of the prospects for peace in Northern...' A car sped by, neighbours called to each other and slammed doors, and the man cleared his throat. 'What do you think of the prospects for peace...' A taxi stopped with the engine juddering and the driver jumped out with a delivery of flowers. My father was either distracted or bored by the glitches, his elbow rising over the top of his ear and head, his fingers dancing. 'What are the prospects...' the man started again, bobbing his microphone. The camera wobbled. I was watching my sister watching them, big-eyed and mouth ajar. She turned back to the house. 'Why does that man keep asking Papa the same question? Doesn't he know the answer? Is he stupid?'

The crowd at these parties was never just British. It seemed that all the other nationalities were represented too, or at least a lot of them, and if not by name they were referred to as 'the Italians', 'the Chinese', 'the Canadians', 'the South Africans'. It was something to do with my mother's background and the way it mixed with my father's work that all the embassy people came along. The South Africans I knew lived in the great big house where the hill descended on the way to Holland Park. Its high walls and the wide pavement usually carried graffiti like 'BOYCOTT

SOUTH AFRICA' and 'NO APARTHEID'. This house, where on a summer's day you could hear tennis balls pop from the garden as you passed by, was cheek by jowl with the school we were not allowed to go to because my father thought we would be bullied, as well as badly educated and possibly bullied for evermore as a result.

One year the Russians brought a present with them to our party, a sleek blue box adorned with silver letters spelling out Garrards, in which were nestled a pair of gold-lined silver cream and sugar bowls. My father ignored it, but my mother was taken aback with embarrassment at

Before a summer party: my father and sisters (dressed in kimonos he brought back from Japan), taken from the drawing-room balcony

the size, or rather the weight, of this gift. The Russians, or Soviets, as people then called them, still had the hammer and sickle on their flag, but the man on the news with the birthmark running over his scalp was clearly up to something in high places.

Each year, I wanted to meet David Owen, who I thought was by far the most debonair politician. Admittedly, the competition was not stiff, what with all the jowls and protuberant eyebrows that seemed to get stragglier as Mrs Thatcher's aura brightened. But I was also fascinated by Neil Kinnock, as he seemed to combine passion with reserve. A Welsh accent, ginger, and leader of the opposition – here was a man of courage. I never saw Margaret Thatcher, despite her reported attendance among the throng of pinstripe, billowing skirts, stabbing cocktail sticks and whirling cigarette smoke.

〜

'Do you think this country should join the Exchange Rate Mechanism?' was one favourite question my father asked my friends if they came for dinner, as though he were asking what their favourite colour was. There was no simple opening gambit; a subject was always brought to the table to be discussed. We didn't have that many friends round, but I had one who came over a lot. My constant friend was called Emily. She greeted my father with embarrassed nerves at first, but then a laughing shuffle of relief that she was being flattered and taken seriously, consulted on a question that was in the news and divided the country.

His questions were not always political though, and not always obvious. 'How many cats do you think there are in England?' or 'What do you think the difference is between the number of pets and the number of farm animals in the country?' Those ones were good for debating and guessing games for anyone young or old, though we couldn't match the facts he could produce, on the history of the Treaty of Rome, say, but equally on offbeat but telling phenomena – for instance the French being great dog importers. The French particularly liked to get their dogs from England, and forecasts predicted that the French dog population might double by the year 2000. I was always struck by my father's ability to sit still in an upright chair for hours at a time and read. The masses of pages he consumed went into conversations like this. What could be even more disorientating than the odd nuggets of knowledge shuttling like skittles in our young minds was his willingness always to turn a subject the other way by question and analysis. Asking the questions was just as important as the answers, and more fool the one who thought the answers could be relied on to stay the same.

As we were growing up, it was Emily who took me out of the dourness that could sometimes drown things at home. It took me a long time to realise it was not only me who could be gloomy – the house had a gloomy aspect too. 'Don't leave unnecessary lights on,' my father sometimes hissed as he crossed a landing. When I was little, he once found me reading on my own upstairs, and asked, 'Why are you sitting in the dark?' There was a reason why, though I didn't have a ready answer, a physical reason but also a more internalised one. A child accepts the contours of their landscape, however uncomfortable. The shadow we sometimes felt constraining us was my father's slack time, when the embers of his public life simmered, ready ing to spark again, layered darkly over the fierce moods he just about held in check.

By contrast, my friend Emily's nature was unstoppably sunny, not particularly self-confident but unself-conscious, loud, clownish and extremely likeable. She had moved to England from Spain at the age of eight, and kept up the belief that her father stayed behind because of his work, rather than that her parents were divorcing, long after she realised otherwise. She idolised her father, a happy-go-lucky family-loving Malagan. But he had a dark streak that made him prone to outbursts of plate-throwing and short-term amnesia. The pieces of this story came out in the years we were friends, without her ever saying as much. We had to accept, without wanting to admit, that for that reason her mother could not live with her father any more.

It saddened my friend enormously to leave Spain and to leave him, but Emily very rarely let this show. Her way was to jump out of bed in the morning, scamper over to the sleeping boxer dog in his basket, do a mad dance of affection with him, before turning up Capital Radio, singing in the shower – 'She wore a raspberry beret' – and prancing around naked before throwing on a body suit and jeans with the ease of the dancer she was. This was far from the way it was in our house, where the voices of the *Today* programme on the 'wireless' trailed after my father as he trod up and down the narrow stairs, fending youngsters away from his path with vibes that we didn't understand but knew we couldn't cross.

Emily and I caught the Number 9 bus home from school together every day. We preferred to stay at her house where often only her older sister was left to look after her, her mother seeing to business in Spain. Sharing Wotsits and fruit pastilles, we developed our own way of talking, putting the accents on our words in all the wrong places and finding this very funny and original. Our other, rather more disgusting habit was tapping out tunes on our teeth by flicking our fingernails at them, a technique at which we were adept. For some reason – because we were firm friends and because of the mother who had traitorously told her father that enough was enough – she didn't mind staying at my house. In a strange way, she enjoyed the eccentricity of my father challenging her to talk about things nobody else gave her credit with understanding. She had always been known as the naughty one, the clumsy one, when she wasn't dancing, falling into punishments by accident and inspiring the contempt of teachers by laughing about it afterwards. I was always known as the good one, but I had as much or more capacity for breaking the rules; I just seemed to get away with it better. Together, however, to the disappointment of our teachers, we carried off our punishments without caring and were no worse off for it.

In the small Catholic school we went to in central London, the custom was to pray before our Religious Studies lessons. The teacher asked the class at the beginning whether there was anyone in particular we wanted to pray for – a reckless move with a group of girls breaking into adolescence, stuck inside all day making the round of a set of small classrooms. We might also have come up from spending our lunch hour in the music room, a windowless room in the basement where we left the lights off and rigged up a Ouija board, as another favourite pastime of ours was 'freaking each other out'. Inevitably, back upstairs under the strip lighting of day, the most common request was to pray for our parents. This was often followed by an emotional outburst about how we were praying only because they might die one day and we couldn't take the pressure, and why did God think we could, and who said He did anyway? The day came when Emily's beloved boxer, who we took down the Hammersmith towpath together every Saturday morning, got sick. She asked the teacher if we could pray for Myrtie. As we were inseparable, we were both taken aside at the end of the lesson so that the teacher could explain to us that there was no point praying for Myrtie because when he died he wouldn't go to Heaven. 'Because dogs don't have souls,' she concluded.

I still find it remarkable that this woman remained unmoved by the weeping and blubbering unleashed in front of her, the noisy defence not just of dogs but of love, friendship, pre-breakfast walks, games of chase and bowls of food. At the same time, it was a demonstration to me of the power of spontaneous affection, of being at one with your instincts, of not prefixing every feeling with the thought that it's not as simple as that. This was the ideal that my father set before me, not in so many words but in the viewpoints and qualifications that always danced around a conversation with him. It was almost a cult of objective thought driven – so he seemed to suggest—by common sense and just part of being civilised. But it meant always pushing to a logical conclusion, with no time for the indulgence of sentimental whim. To be so free of prejudice was inspiring, but to be free of irrational attachment – whether to the peso or franc on holiday, to your dog, or your desire for the same shiny Walkman as all your friends had – was toughening.

Being part of Europe was a passionate belief of my father's, though never polemically expressed. It was at least in part his experience of meeting my mother while he was reporting in Paris that made him such a committed European, and certainly the influence of their first years together in Germany. He had none of the prejudice against the French my mother grumbled about if she had time to look through the pages of *The Times* – even though he had plenty of opportunity for cheap shots given the way his parents-in-law ostracised d him. His cultured exterior made it hard to know whether it was hurtful, or how hurtful it was to him, not to be visiting the Picasso museum with us in Antibes or eating peaches in the shade of the pepper tree, playing the Lotto and watching the epic miniseries *The Life of Verdi*. That TV series dominated one summer for us, and was a hit sensation across France in the 80s, perhaps England as well, with a pan-European cast including Burt Lancaster. I knew he would have loved it too. One year or another, when we got home as autumn was rolling in, he mentioned his trip to Edinburgh to see all manner of fringe theatre and comedy. So he did lead a life of pleasure and entertainment away from us, and I wondered at the discipline, or otherwise, of his doing this without his family.

His conviction that the only factual base for anything was an economic one sat closely with the idea that there is no fixed moral compass. Capital punishment was barbaric, but he brought us into the ambiguities, asking, 'How many people in your class would have to get a gun, before you decided you had to get one too?'

His cast of mind meant that contradictions did not exist where superficial judgments might suggest they did. Margaret Thatcher apparently once said that most *Financial Times* journalists were the sort of intellectual lefties who also wrote for *Marxism Today*. A subscription to this magazine came through our door, and my father was vocal on the subject of why it was very good and why it mattered. But there was also a vague rumour that he acted as an advisor to Margaret Thatcher, so close was he to events in Westminster. Sometimes the misconception is made that the *Financial Times* is a right-wing paper, probably because it analyses the movement of money. My father was clearly uninterested in money, which added to this ambiguity about what he really thought, or what he really felt.

My father could never have been a revolutionary because he saw too many sides of the question. But I always wondered whether somewhere deep down he was a Marxist – he definitely always brought things back to economics as the engine of politics and social change. But somewhere in that same mix there was conservatism, with a small 'c'. No need to destroy for the sake of it, no need to go wild calling out illogical slogans like the 68ers, any more than calling for peace when war was necessary. He was out of step with the 80s in so many ways, and with the brash pinstriped men of Fleet Street who were the modern face of journalism. This, too, I thought, was something that caused him pain. He liked the joke about teabag-drinking Marxists – 'Proper tea is theft' – but those original ideals of the left seemed to interest him more, at least as an intellectual standard, than the growing concerns of many of his peers: paying less tax to afford private schools and skiing holidays. At the same time, he was unmoved by the counterculture, unimpressed by the naïve leftism of knee-jerk pacifists, or people who thought it was all right to 'opt out'. If we whined or complained, a shrug and a snort that we were 'bolshy' was the usual reply. Even if we didn't understand what it meant, we knew we should get over being self-indulgent and losing our sense of humour, in other words, our sense of perspective. He was sceptical of by-lines; though he had one for his 'Politics Today' column and his book and theatre reviews. The leader column was still a sacred space, a privileged viewpoint assuming a mantle of objectivity without the agenda of self-advancement. Unsigned too, because it was sometimes a collaboration, it was another column he took on, renaming it from the original and dated 'Men and Matters' to the inclusive 'Observer'. He disliked the growing fashion for photographs next to by-lines, even though as a newspaperman he was interested in the possibilities of colour and printing technology. This perhaps was a contradiction in him: the rift where he began to separate from his times.

He might also ask what our friends' parents did, and often found out that the parents involved were leading separate lives. When Emily tried to explain what her father did, she stumbled, as the only thing clear to her was that he had worked for the ailing IBM, pronounced

as though he considered my sisters and I to be spoiled by the growing materialism of the age. Even asking for the right kit for school was fraught with restraint. Why should we need a tracksuit and a leotard *and* a swimsuit? When he was at school, all the boys lined up and plunged in with no trunks at all and no complaints. English private schools, where we were sent for our secondary education, require a whole new alphabet of accessories. Our bowlers were soft and bruised from use, our boaters were pleated from being sat on and boxed up in past holidays. Our summer dresses had the obsolete puffed sleeves rather than the cuff of the new ones. The compromise was based on the belief we wouldn't get a good enough education at our local school, so we were placed among the children of industry, finance, oil and shipping. My school education was never as strong as the one I unwittingly received at home from my father – as that taught me not what, but how to think. This gave me a fortitude that came in useful in this narrow social mix, where we took the lessons but none of the extras that went along with that way of life.

It was a pragmatic decision, and we struggled to keep up with it. The year my sister was expelled from her school happened to be the same year I refused to go back to the claustrophobic Catholic house in Knightsbridge. It had turned into open warfare between a pubescent gangland and its enemy, the geeks, and I refused to fit into either camp. I had never told my parents how much I hated going to school, and how Emily, my closest friend in the world, had suddenly fallen horribly prey to teenage girl groupthink. We had always been friends across certain divides, one reason our friendshipwas so strong and vital to us. When I gave in to a tearful outburst about it, my father arranged for me to go to a bigger, better school, without my realising at the time he had already paid for the forthcoming year at the old school. It was evident because of the strain, but he never drew attention to the fact that, because of my sister's expulsion and my refusal to go back, he ended up paying five lots of school fees for us that year.

My mother no longer took her stall in Portobello Market, but she sometimes took something to Christie's auction house to get a valuation, which she then thought about for a while. Years later, she told me that the autumn when my sister and I moved schools, she had taken the book to be valued – the bilingual album with the Picasso drawing of the poet dressed up as the don of the bullfight in a sleeve bound into its spine. She had also once put it among the other bits on her bric-a-brac stall, inviting people to pick it up and look at the pictures of famous artists and literary men. People came past, picked it up and had a flick through – nice pictures, but it was in a foreign language, two in fact, so they always put it back without bothering to ask the price. A curio that happened to contain a key to where my parents started out, and the story in pictures and words of a poet called Apollinaire who became the vessel for so much longing, the book took on an immeasurable value to me. It is probably unreasonable to feel sad on behalf of Apollinaire that after his childhood on the Mediterranean, he did not go away to Antibes or Collioure or Céret in the summer months as all his friends did to paint and to feel the light and air. Almost every time, he stayed in Paris, working. He was a journalist, and journalists never switch off. Their bank balances and the endless run of events marching on prevent them. Perhaps something in their disposition too cuts them off from casual time spent with other people, not devoted to thinking and working.

⤥

That third side of my father was that he was so resistant to being categorised. He was not a Tory, but being a lefty at that time came with its own problems of outdated associations and naïveté. For him, as a journalist, these questions were irrelevant anyway. Analysis was inflected by plenty of opinion, or rather by a highly informed point of view, but not by personal bias, and not explicitly. Still, I wondered if part of what tormented him was the division that was occurring from a widely followed Left to a more popular centre-right ground, with a pragmatically updated surface and, it arguably turned out, a self-aggrandising agenda within. But it is easy to divide the world according to these sorts of crude moral alignments, like Orwell's 'four legs good' and 'two legs bad'. No wonder so many revolutions failed. Thinking for yourself is much harder. I remember my father dismissing lawyers as 'intellectual cowards' as their work was based on learning rules and texts, more than on individual analysis. Bang went another perfectly sensible career choice for me. But you have to grow up, leave the anarchist follies of your youth behind, the egalitarian dreams, the corpse of your father and your days.

My mother had struck off on a limb of her own in marrying my father. But while we made a new and sep arate unit in London, the two sides of the family mutually ignoring the other, we still cleaved to the maternal side. My mother still played the role of daughter, visiting and bringing small presents to her parents in all the holidays, looking after them as they got older. In all the times we were not with my father, and were with my mother and grandparents instead, I could never comfortably believe that their homes were my home too, that they were my family as much as my father was. Blood is thicker than the half-blood of grandchildren, and my grandmother did not seem capable of believing or conveying to us otherwise. After all, she had already rejected one of her own sons. It was as though in some ways we were always treading a fine line, part and not part of the same family. Since then, I have recreated my own notion of home, of being at home and finding comfort in that place.

I've had the courage to look behind me
The corpses of my days
Mark my path and I weep for them
Some of them rotting in Italian churches
Or in the copses where the lemon trees grow
They fruit and they flower
At once and in the same season
Other days wept before collapsing in taverns
Where ardent flowers garland
The eyes of a brown lady inventing poetry
And the roses of electricity open again
In the garden of my memory

Forgive my ignorance
Forgive me for no longer knowing the ancient game of
     verse

Lines from a poem written in Paris in 1907, one of a trio
Apollinaire produced in an intense period of creativity
in him and his painter friends. Picasso was starting on
'Les Demoiselles d'Avignon' in the privacy of his studio,
where Apollinaire visited him every day. Apollinaire
called this poem 'The Betrothal' and dedicated it to
Picasso, who was a witness to the poet's wedding the
year before his death in the flu epidemic of 1918.

After our early summers as young children when we stayed two whole months in the South, and my cousins were often with us, the house began to put up with us less. We outgrew the straw hats we had been so excited to find again after a year's absence. The buckets and spades stayed in the garage as now we went only to the jetty beaches with ladders into the sea and no sand to play on. I found the scruffy orange bear I had lost in the garden one summer before, and though it still seemed like amazing luck he had survived, we had already shared our last expedition on an equal footing. My grandfather now stayed in the house at all times, hooked up to his oxygen in the dining room. That and his adjoining study were made into his quarters, so he no longer had to contend with stairs. He was in fine health mentally and physically except that he could not breathe unaided. The thin green fluorescent tube that pumped oxygen into his prominent nostrils was his line to survival.

We sometimes arrived quailing from carsickness, after extending the journey as long as we could, through territory between my mother's husband and her parents in which she felt herself free and independent again. For miles on the roadsides between villages, away from the tedium of motorways, vineyards tracked their neat long lines. Close up, the branches were as twisted and gnarled as grand old trees sucking the goodness from red earth. Purple grapes as big as plums hung from them in perfect cone-shaped bunches. With a surprising amount of puffing, we hacked one off to try. The skins of the fruit were so thick they needed chewing. They had a texture and richness more akin to an animal product. Inside the grapes was nectar that produced as much thirst as it quenched. We ate our fill, until our stomachs turned with the sugars and we spewed dark-red liquid from the car window onto the roadside.

Not long after we arrived at the house, grimy from travelling, we heard our grandfather sighing almost with physical pain at this story of our eating grapes stolen from the vineyards. He did not come and greet us, but hovering outside the salon, we heard his repeated '*Ah la la, ça alors, c'est pas possible*' from his chair, followed by my grandmother's piercing drawl, 'Pierre, darling', designed against her nature to placate him. Our offence in taking and eating ripe grapes destined for wine was reported to us second and third hand. I had never heard or seen my grand father anything like so angry and thoroughly disappointed with us before, and my grandmother the one trying to appease him. He did not come and sit with us before dinner and he never said it to us directly. The oddly

disturbing experience of the spectacular grapes so delicious they made us sick began to feel even more wrong.

As dusk was falling, my grandmother brought a
saucer of milk out to place under a bush at the far side
of the terrace. 'Pipioule! Pipioule!' she called. She had
befriended a hedgehog, named him and tempted him with
milk each evening. He came out on the terrace, pointy
snout roaming and sniffing, and blindly dunked his head
into the shallow bowl. She had the expectation of certain
birds who came to peck at the vines in the early mornings.
All of a sudden I got a picture of my grandmother alone,
talking to the animals. Her face lit up as she called for the
hedgehog, gently demonstrating the secrets of the garden.
It was strange to feel this premonition of the future in our
midst, the house emptied of people and my grandmother
still watering the agapanthus as the sun went down, but
not bothering to light the citronella lanterns outside as
she shut the glass-and-iron doors against the night. The
terrace was still laid with glass and silverware, the balco-
nies still overlooked the sea. Lined up on a chest in size
order were the immaculate green textured globes of the
urchin shells my cousins and I had collected for her when
we were little from the bottom of the sea. More and more,
I thought of the 'secret sorrow' that Apollinaire alluded
to in his poems, and the strange image of his 'heart hung
from the lemon trees'.

It was too much for my grandmother to come with us
to the beach every day, because her patience was thin,

not because she lacked physical strength. Maybe only when we left the house could she sit with her husband and talk in peace, able to show a softer face. Maybe they reflected on the contract they had made, a hard and fast bond to each other, in their heydays allowing them each plenty of independence but no ties to their original families. We had to be back at five o'clock for tea, then baths and helping before dinner at eight. Time felt as though it had stood still all day, until our arrival triggered the rotation of trays and silver and carafes and covered dishes again. We did not see my grandfather until drinks before dinner, but in the preparation in between, as my grandmother passed through the interconnecting rooms of the ground floor, she visited him in his curtained space, picking up a continuum of dialogue between them. I heard the snatches of what seemed a painfully familiar but long-withheld discussion. '*A la fin de ma vie*,' my grandfather's rasping voice came, '*nous nous sommes brouillés avec ma famille*.' He was dying, and now he realised how far, through his career and his wife, he had become cut off from the family he once had.

My mother varied the day by taking us to walk in the lavender hills above Antibes, or to the tiny island of Porcerole you could see across the bay on the clearest days. We also went to the Picasso museum, every year and often more than once. Originally called the Château Grimaldi, it resembles a geometric rock sculpture punctuated with medieval slit windows. A small slice of stone terraced garden is caught between its sheer walls and the wall plunging straight down to the sea. The château was turned into a museum in 1925, when it began to be called the Musée Grimaldi, but in those days, before Picasso's time, it had housed only an unremarkable collection of archaeological finds. In 1945, Picasso came to stay in Antibes with his lover Françoise Gilot. Struggling to make good use of the large stone spaces of the château, the museum's curator loaned the building to Picasso for use as a studio as long as he stayed in Antibes. Several unadorned chambers on three levels hang with the works of the master, with photographs of him at work in the château or the famous one of him standing holding a white parasol aloft as his beautiful lover strides forward adored by him and the sun. I know that beach where they basked, footsteps down the hill, the light and air like magic. He looks like the cat that got the cream.

The painting I liked most of all at the Picasso museum is a massive one of two dimensionally flat but very fat women running along the beach. Sturdy silhouettes, snout-like noses, one of them upturned to the sky, their fat fingers and elephant legs spread out close to the edges of the canvas. Their hair streaks out behind them, and their arms stretch in all directions, their hands loosely clasped in a spontaneous gesture of friendship. It is painted in deep-rose and flesh colours, a primitive contrast with the sea and sky in blues that compete for brightness. Despite the heft of the two women, they seem to be leaping down the beach in the open sun-drenched air, absolutely free and weightless. They are running along the sand just down the road. They seemed like the essence of the place. As I looked at that picture every year, it seemed to me as if Picasso was owned by that coastline and the old village on its rocky verge, and all of us who were there owned a piece of him. In the corridors of the museum were cases of documents, extra information for the boffins and the bored. I knew the handwriting on those postcards, and the people in those photographs. I knew those fragments of poetry, and I felt I knew the poet who put as much care into making a truffle risotto as composing a sonnet in alexandrines arranged like a fountain on the page. 'Winkles codfish multiple suns and urchins of the setting planet' – those signs and objects appear in poems and paintings by one and the other, like the wistful and mysterious harlequins they were both obsessed by. Those poems were by Apollinaire, Picasso's compadre of the *belle époque.* As the web of my family stretched more thinly, the poems he left behind started to become for me a bridge both back to it and forward.

≈

'In a house not so far from here, yes, a villa not unlike this one.' Through the arches of the terrace, the crickets sang in the night, and I watched the lizards against the folded plasterwork of the ceiling, my breath synchronised with the infinitesimal beat of their flanks as they paused at an unseen threat before darting for the corners. My grandmother was talking at the table. 'They were giving a party that weekend. Or Madame Marchal was. She was a widow. The gardener was Moroccan. The neighbours used him too.' Her eyes darting around and settling on nobody in particular, she filled the space between the courses as the plates were changed, more dishes brought. Talking and talking irrespective of comment, fiddling with her dessert spoon and fork, only something outside her order of things would interrupt her, and then we would reel with the storm. After lamb brochettes or chicken roasted with thyme and preserved lemon, with either rice or *rissolé* potatoes, chopped the size of dice

The house in Antibes

and flavoured with sprigs of rosemary from the garden, came the salad, never cut with a blade, but only torn if the leaves were too big, and then folded carefully by knife and fork into a mouthful, 'no bigger than a cherry', said my grandmother. She demonstrated by making a wrinkled round of her lips. I realised everyone was rapt by the bizarre story she was telling. 'It was they who found her. Yes. On the walls of the *cave*, written in blood, 'OMAR M'A TUER.' My grandmother gasped at her own words and threw her hands up to indicate the scandal, the crisis: Madame Marchal, a woman minding her own business at home, giving parties and doing her best, dead in her own garden, killed by the man to whom she had given a job.

The story reverberated across the dinner table, seeping into the shadowy corners of the terrace and the garden beyond, where men could be hiding in wait. On the car radio and the news before dinner, the scandal echoed across the region, across France. Was it racism in our midst again? Was it revenge for France's colonial abuses? Did the government, the rich, the innocent have it coming? Or was it a set-up, an individual caught in a far more personal feud? My grandmother seemed more indomitable than ever, impervious to threat and no doubt aware she would outlive her own generation, and certainly her husband. She relished the scandal, and I was divided in my sympathy for her, wondering what was happening to Omar and his family as they were hunted for justice. But more fundamentally, I was divided in that I already found it so hard to forgive my grandmother. I could not accept her tantrums as another side of her charisma, and could not easily love her. She had excluded my father, and my resemblance to him marked the way she saw me too. To her, the only point in being an Englishman was to be knighted, and the only point in working for a newspaper was to run it or better still to own it. She represented so much that was anathema to him that it seemed to me a betrayal to go along with her erratic affections. After all, she represented just the same anathema to him and by extension to me, but he didn't play the bully.

Near the bedroom window of the blue room at the house in Antibes stood an ancient and stubborn citrus tree. It produced a fruit rarely, a flash of orange that came with much labour after the spring frosts. Next to it was a giant cedar, its branches spiralling from a foot off the ground and upwards, making a ladder leading to the balcony at the back of the house. One night, half asleep beneath the open shutters, I thought I heard the breathing of some-body approaching. Each time it stopped, the branches of the cedar outside creaked. Each time the creaking stopped, I could hear two soft breaths slowly exhaled into the dark. A leap from the branches of the cedar tree could land you on the balcony that led to the room my grandfather slept in. But he no longer slept up in the master bedroom, and in any case was now at the clinic having his lungs cleared. I still don't know if I heard the creaking of the cedar and a man's breath. I used to imagine I was much more awake than I actually was in the night – the mosquito bites all over me in the morning were testimony to that.

When I woke, my mother was shouting from her room – her jewellery, money, our passports. They had gone. My grandmother had already left the house and would be back any moment with my grandfather. The gravel crunched. Two cars rolled into the drive, one my grandmother's, the other would be bearing my grandfather with his equipment. My grandmother was opening the iron-and-glass entrance doors, leading the way, when she stopped. She took one look ahead of her, snapping out of a trance of worry brought on by hospital visits, and back into being mistress of the house. A weird unformed gasp left her lips and her arms flapped in front of her as she faltered from the step and into the space of the hallway. We, the three girls, were halfway down the wide staircase in our nightdresses, our eyes transfixed, half ready to run back out of sight and half preparing to rush to her aid. 'The clock!' she cried. 'The grandfather clock! Thieves!' Heading to her desk with emergency resolve, she started rummaging through the drawers, throwing pens and folders aside. 'Get some paper, draw the hands, the numerals. He mustn't see!'

There were marauders at work in the dark gardens of the houses set back from the beach. They were ruthless, it was well known. My grandmother moved with frantic speed, sticking bits of paper together and crudely drawing the clock face. She plucked a random hour and minute from the air, scoring the numerals and ornate hands on paper with a felt-tip pen. Opening the fat glass door of the clock, she stuck the mock face to its inside. It should have housed the domed porcelain face set with Roman numerals and metal hands, a solid moon over heavy and intricate workings behind. Thieves had taken the inside of the clock, but the clock itself was as big as a man and too large to move. It was from Les Vallières. Its tall central compartment showed the pendulum had now vanished. The oblong wooden interior, with none of the varnish of the outside casement, was feeble and somehow threatening without its contents. My grandfather was carried in then by two nurses. He was lying immobile but breathing on a stretcher, narrow green tubes extending from his nostrils, his oxygen cylinders wheeling precariously behind him. We looked in a mixture of horror and confusion at my grandmother's attempt to hide him from the enormous empty clock.

I don't know whether my grandfather was asleep or unconscious on his stretcher. He had taken a turn for the worse, but he still lived on, reading, thinking, sitting, joining us for the eight o'clock news and the Lotto before dinner, taken back in his room. It seemed the more my grandfather retreated into the clutches of a terminal illness, the more the dimensions of my grandmother's stormy nature grew. She was like a dragon guarding her docile companion in his lair. The two of them were set more and more decisively apart from the families they started off with, his seven brothers and sisters and their families only a few hours away, possibly taking their holidays along the Riviera too. We never saw them. Since my grandfather's retirement from the Ministry, the circuit between Paris, the Midi and the Loire was what they did, and though we knew of my grandfather's childhood at the château in the middle of France's breadbasket, the hordes of cousins and the chocolate factory that was still running, together he and my grandmother had turned their backs on it, as my grandmother soon would on us.

Poem about the rain, printed with letters in ragged descending diagonals like drops falling on a window pane, written at the resort of Deauville in 1914, just before the news broke that France was at war.

ENGLAND

There were a lot of stairs in our house in London, the zigzag of short flights heading down from the front hall permanently in shadow. The people who lived there before and the servants who worked there in the past were clearly smaller than we are now, at least smaller than many of my parents' friends. My father was five foot eleven – an average height for a man – but he was of slender build. Our family fitted the tight dimensions fine but I always thought a brother would not have fared so well. Some of the most important events seemed to happen on the stairs.

One stray photograph of my father sitting on them with my older sister crouching behind him looks like a picture of filial affection in all its simple mystery. I remember poring over it dumbly, as it was not the image of our daily affections. I don't have the classic memory of the child of warring parents, sitting on the stairs outside a kitchen or drwaing room listening to them argue, because my sisters did this in the early days and as the youngest I didn't feel the need to. I didn't know what they were really arguing about; it was all part of the shapeless grey swill of tension and it felt like old news to me. Rows that once blared had settled into the unspoken rhythm of marriage, a knot that is too complicated to be undone, however uncomfortably tied. The memory of the single argument we sisters had with my father about his family and the way he lied about it – or in fairness, withheld this from us – took place on the stairs outside his study.

I was twelve or thirteen, sitting on the floor by the bookshelves in the drawing room flicking through the smooth, thin outsize pages of a *Who's Who*. I was looking up Margaret Drabble, as I had just read *The Millstone* and several other of her novels and was writing a school essay about her. I thought I might as well look up my father, and see what it said about him. I thought he might have a listing, since so many people he knew did, and I was right. There he was, 'Journalist'. Typically, he hadn't added any hobbies or interests; no opera, cooking or collecting model aeroplanes for him; no deliberate personal embellishments. But then there was something else; a mere couple of facts but they were completely unexpected and redefined what I took to be who we were, our family: '1st marriage; 1 daughter, m. dissolved. 2nd marriage, 3 daughters.' This was strange information. I wondered if maybe I had had a shade of this knowledge once, but I couldn't be sure.

It emerged on the stairs, and it was pretty definitely around Christmas time, when we were all in the house together for an unusually extended time. The memory is blurred at the edges, partly because while being angry with my father and wanting to know the truth – or rather wanting to have the reassurance of him telling the truth to us, no matter its object – I sympathised with how he didn't want to have this conversation. He didn't want to have it with children; with his children; with anyone. He was impatient with it, callous and contemptuous of the need to know. It made him uncomfortable. It pained him; maybe it tormented him. Perhaps it was the invisible link that drove him mercilessly forward, out of the house each night or behind his study door, never breaking for a holiday or to see where chance took him. My middle sister led the charge, levelling the accusations of betrayal and secrecy – it was not clear to me about what. As much as I was pushing to know, I recoiled from putting him on the spot. He was looking sideways, in the doorway of his study, unable to respond, and I suppose it fizzled out, like so many arguments when the person who is the target of fury refuses to give back in kind. He had as much fury as the rest of us though, against his nature, I think. My mother I know took the brunt of it even though we absorbed its constant muted reverberations in the way our household operated.

For a long time, I saw this discovery of my father's other child and former wife in a useful light – or I resolved to. Certainly I was confused by it, and also burdened because this was more vague knowledge that could not be shared. But I argued to myself that it was a reason for how things

was some comfort in this conventional explanation: he did that so he was like this to us. Even as a twelve- or thirteen-year-old, in the wake of this discovery, I was suspicious of such a unilateral interpretation.As his daughter, I knew that people's behaviour was not explained like this in a simple causal sequence. Since his death, I have seen it more charitably, with less anger, and remembered his vulnerability as much as his extreme independence. It has become much more possible to think of him in relation to himself rather than in relation to me – to acquire that objectivity he so esteemed. I have come to sympathise with this rupture as part of what tormented him. He made a mistake, but that is no way to summarise falling in love with my mother. He had an affair. He absented himself from the country behind the calling of his career, during the four years it took for the rupture to settle – perhaps – and to come back in a new formation fitted piecemeal over the old. Later, and no doubt under pressure from his new wife with the three babies in quick succession, he failed to broker a situation that could accommodate the past. I think this made him suffer; it was part of what made him suffer. It was one of the flawed exchanges life was full of.

Yet there was still the residue of him being a man capable of reckless acts, not bound by the rules of consensus. When I looked at the uplift of his face in profile in the doorway of his study, a zone always blurred at the edges by the billows of cigarette smoke, I saw the pride maintained there. Why should I answer for myself to you, to anyone? It is the fate of people close to us – husbands and wives must withstand this down side – that we're not always able to hold our heads high. We see the crack in the mask, the effort to keep up one's story. I never thought of my parents as invulnerable, or as great by virtue of being older, like the playground boast of a dad who is fifty, no, a *hundred*! That they were a few years older than other people's parents simply brought their mortality closer. But despite there being no precise moment when I suddenly recognised that childish illusion for what it is, it was still disturbing to see their vulnerabilities co-existing with their public faces. Prior knowledge of the mistakes we children might be drawn to repeat ourselves is frightening. I was sometimes frightened too by the personal demon of being outside the consensus, possibly incapable of the conventional bonds of marriage.

When they spent their four years in Germany then, the absence was long enough to forget about a former wife and a young child, or was it? The periods overlap, the crisis in one relationship caused by the beginning of the other. It was the career break that let the personal off the hook, or pushed it from view. Then there were new children eating up space, airtime, money. When they started coming, three turned up in as many years. The wall of the pregnant belly was raised again, and each time harder to surmount, creating a steeper divide between public and private selves. Our English grandparents too may have been divided in their loyalties, drawn to protect the welfare of their first granddaughter, enlisted to siphon money to the firstborn behind the scenes.

Whether your parents love each other is probably a question asked by teenagers all over the place. Along with 'Am I really adopted?' (No – the resemblances are far too apparent), 'Am I really a fantastic being from another dimension?' and 'Could I have been an amazing dancer or singer or painter if only my parents had understood and nurtured my talent?' I wondered this about them, within the limited bounds of a presumption of the silliness, sentimentality, and frankly the unimportance of a question like that. So what? seemed to be the message. Love? – We have better things to think about. Those aren't the aspirations of life, the ideal destiny. This was something much more aggressively focused on events in the world, on work, on the mind, the thinking mind that is, shaken free in a fallacy that it can be unaffected by feeling. In this promise of freedom was a trap, where I witnessed my father's suffering, and I was caught in it. This fallacy can stifle your better nature. Love suppressed leaks out in hostile form.

My parents never mythologised their story of falling in love on the Pont Mirabeau – they barely ever spoke about their meeting or their pasts. My mother only dropped in passing that it was love at first sight, a love to end all other loves. I am left with a few insubstantial facts, and the poem I read as a teenager – 'Under the Pont Mirabeau runs the Seine' – with its lullaby rhythm and deceptively simple lines. Its internal rhymes and repeated vowels, and its hackneyed paradox – 'The days go by, I remain' – put it in danger of verging on the contrived in French, except that it is not contrived at all. Apollinaire made the sounds lap like the waves he loved, though the shores of his childhood leave a physical mark on his work only rarely. The sounds of the poem are too dependent on the French words to lend themselves well to English translation, but they have been set to music many times by both English and French singers, and to me this poem seems as close to a universal language as might be possible.

After the Christmas when the story of his past – known at least to some extent by my sisters already – came out, we went walking in Holland Park. If it snowed we took tea trays to the hill that is now bordered by a Japanese garden, and sat on them to launch ourselves down the runway. The oddest sight of all that year on the edge of the flower garden, where peacocks stray from the wooded edges, was an albino bird. I was sitting on the bench with my sisters, pausing at the nothingness in the aftermath of revelation, when the peacock came into view. Buttery white all over with shining red eyes, it was identical to the others in everything but its lack of colour; and we knew at least we three had witnessed the same thing and here we still were.

A woman weeping
Eh oh ah!
The soldiers marching
Eh oh ah!
A lockkeeper fishing
Eh oh ah!
Trenches blanching
Eh oh ah!
Shells farting
Eh oh ah!
Matches that wouldn't strike
Eh oh ah!
And all
in me
> *has changed*
>> *so much*
>> *All*
>> *But my love*
>>> *Eh oh ah!*

'Mutation', written by Apollinaire from his station at Nîmes in 1915.

FRANCE

I was held in a feeling of suspension; nothing to say, nothing to do. It was too soon to go over happy memor ies, too final to articulate the sorrow, too trivial even to say that was it that we felt. Emily, my inseparable friend, the one I'd had sleepovers with three or four nights out of every seven, was killed instantly in a car crash one Saturday night while we were at university. Her death was the purest shock, and gave the crudest sense of unfinished business. The argument I'd had on the phone the night before with my boyfriend, which meant I was distracted and late and failed to phone her, was such a stupid thing to have got in the way. The reassurance I made to myself to call her some time during the next few days, as it was her nineteenth birthday, so we would definitely talk and catch up, swap stories about university and plan our next London adventure, was empty. When our mutual friend, the third in our three from ten years back, came to my door in tears at ten o'clock on Sunday morning, I knew all the reassurances I'd made for myself, the drama and distraction were useless, broken toys discarded along the way. The taxi she and a friend had been travelling in to a party started to speed up and swerve. At first it was funny – I could hear the hysterical laughter of her excitement in anticipation of Saturday night – but it got more serious. It got to be nausea-inducing and frightening. The driver was drunk. They grabbed their seat belts too late, or she did. Her friend got away with whiplash, shock and a residue of guilt. But Emily — I don't know what happened in those final moments, though part of my brain continues to insert the scene into a reel that keeps turning.

It was some time, but not long enough, before I felt again the desolate emptiness of expectation after someone dies, that they will somehow reappear from behind a door, or at least visit you in your dreams, and knowing that they will not. But I had one dream then, around the time of her death, and I cannot remember if it was before or after-wards. It was the experience of a girl with her back to me in a shadowy space, its edges lost in the folds of my sleep-drenched mind. She was perhaps less a girl than a statue, but I knew it was her. With her back to me, nude and pale like the statue of the girl with the pitcher of water in the garden in Antibes, half girl half woman, she was turning. She kept on turning, lifting her shoulder, a slight crane of her neck and the glimpse of a quarter-profile, and she kept on turning. She was trying to tell me something, that she was disappearing perhaps, and she kept on turning.

We were a double act known to all our friends. She was the foil for my introspection. Around our dinner table, in the company of my father and the questions he opened our eyes to, she started to believe in other parts of herself and in her own intelligence. I had lost the extrovert side of our pair, the one who had boundless faith in the perfect symmetry of our future lives, bridesmaids at each other's weddings, husbands who were buddies, godmothers to each other's children. And the one who had so much faith in my wisdom and the power of my imagination, far more faith than I had in myself. It seems so unkind that it was *her* life cut short. I've occasionally been able to hear the echo of her laugh in the open face of a stranger.

There I was on the college green again, with the same friends, the same soft spring sunshine and the sounds of chatting and laughter, with the serious undercurrent of young people devoted to their studies peeling off to libraries to fill their minds with the inocuous demands of the week's assignment. I was back from London where I had spoken at Emily's memorial service at the Catholic church we had occasionally been to when growing up. At school we had once been set the task of learning the Beatitudes by heart, and because we spent all our free time playing furiously fast games of Spit, betting with Tutti Frutties or dried pasta, we were incapable of the rote performance we were called on at random to give in our Religious Studies lessons. We were set one of our many joint punishments, this time standing at the foot of the wooden banister at lunchtime in the school's William Morris-papered hallway, attempting to recite the Beatitudes to our teacher. *Blessed are the poor in spirit, for theirs in the kingdom of heaven. Blessed are the meek...*

We had to shovel the words into our short-term memories just before we went to our summons. Emily was too distracted for this, and the teacher's eyes darted between the two of us and hovered in a space between our heads, assessing that one would pass and the other strictly speaking couldn't, but that we would both be excused as it was too much trouble otherwise. I thought about this on the way to the memorial, and the mad rush of Emily's energy, and how complementary we were. I was the owl, and she was the sun, and something about that went into the poem I said for her at the gathering of generations, we teenagers turning into young women bearing the confusion of a blow like this. A blow is no more confusing, really, than a boon like the fabled perfect family, but why would we bother to interrogate that? And why would it interrogate us?

There on the green, I was suspended in the dawning aftermath, the slow beginnings of the stilling of shock – partly a shock, but it also felt like confirmation of an inherent traitorous streak in things. I was coming into a new knowledge nonetheless, and I did not know its dimensions. I was berating my housemate for not doing the washing-up or replacing the teabags when I came back from doing the hardest thing so far in my life – speaking at my best friend's memorial service. I could feel the fierce solace of the sun shining on my bare crossed legs on the grass, my housemate's face twitching with guilt as I sent my quiet volley of words to him across the chattering of the group. He didn't know what to say, and I didn't talk about it again. A phone call came taking me away to the Dean's office: my grandfather was dead – not suddenly, but finally. He had been declining for so long, pulled back from the brink many times with stronger drugs and niftier machines, stays in a near-death state in one of the fancy clinics in the hills in the South of France that feel like something out of a JG Ballard novel. I had to go straight back to London, and then to France.

I don't remember anything about the journey. When we got there, the party was incomplete as ever, made up of us girls, my mother, and the one uncle who had a family of his own with his two daughters. My grandparents' favourite son was either away on a diplomatic mission or somehow unable to get to Antibes in time; the ejected one was either not invited or refused to come. My grandmother was still in charge but much silenced, like a storm that had run its course. I suppose my mother was a buffer between her and the younger generation. They sat together on the other side of a drawn curtain, thick yellow velvet dividing their hushed conversation from us, assembled around a low card table for a cold supper on the other side of it. We hadn't kept in close contact with our cousins over the years, not yet able to see the preciousness of these relationships. My cousin was still in a way a mirror to me, almost exactly the same age and with the shared memories of our closeness as small children. Alarm and bewilderment in her eyes, she almost whispered to me, 'Did your best friend die really recently?' 'Yes. Three weeks ago.' They were silenced by several types of shock, and the awareness that certain subjects were inappropriate to the occasion we had been brought together for.

Somebody shepherded us into the funeral parlour the following day. An unadorned terracotta-tiled room presented a mild surprise, but I registered in a dull way that it seemed an apt anteroom to the crossroads beyond – panacea or anticlimax. My grandfather's body was embalmed in his coffin, beside which there was a stool or two for visitors who wanted to linger. I allowed myself to look briefly, a few seconds boring into him deadpan, wanting to see but not, vaguely ashamed of clocking the trivial and macabre details of the scene, but basically indifferent to qualms. The natural tan of his skin was exaggerated by a layer of smooth make-up and his thin lips receded inwards, only a slight distortion of his living face but enough to give it a slightly grotesque air, florid but beaten. It looked like a drawstring was pulling his face from within, cleaving it tight to his skull. Afterwards

I learned that his lips had been sewn together. We laid wreaths and went out again.

The funeral was small-scale and more sombre for that – furtive, even, despite the guidance of tradition – in the cathedral of old Antibes. I can't remember ever having been there with my grandfather, and nobody came because my grandmother had decided not to put a death notice in the paper in case she had to contend with members of her husband's family. Then we left for the Loire, where the burial would take place in the cemetery outside the village near the old château, and where my diplomat uncle still had his country house at the orangery. My grandmother travelled in the hearse with the open coffin. Perhaps she talked to him about all the harmony and the love expressed in the birthday poems my grandfather used to write for her and read to us over pink champagne brought up from the *cave*. Perhaps that bond, pragmatic though it often seemed, justified their aloneness otherwise. It was strange to see her in the chastened aspect of conventional mourning, black dress, black shawl over her head and clutching a missal, and the same stricken look I had witnessed on my mother when she had come with me to Emily's memorial service three weeks earlier. I was angry with my mother then for donning the mask of somebody else's grief. Now, even more unfairly, I felt angry with her for letting the mask slip again and again, falling over, dropping her Bible, hyperventilating, unable to speak, and showing all the outward symptoms of grief.

On a flat brown field, in an empty country village cemetery where we had only the flimsiest connection, we buried my grandfather alone, his grave adjacent to no one's. That was the last time I went to the Loire.

Not long after finishing university, I found myself visiting my grandmother in Antibes and taking along my current boyfriend. It must have been early or late summer, as it was hot but the sky was unsettled. The house now silent and emptied down to my grandmother alone and the two of us visiting, it felt like the prelude to another, more definite ending. My grandmother had moved into the little apartment where we had always slept as children, and put me in the master bedroom, its large bed divided from the room's sitting area by tasselled curtains decorated with birds perched on bowers. My boyfriend was tall and pale, and she welcomed him with the exclamation, 'You look like a leek!' He laughed, confident in the assumption that old people can be shrugged off as harmless eccentrics. She put him in a room at the other end of the house, so we were tucked away and insulated in different quarters, though my grandmother asked me, 'Does he take a bath? I can't hear the taps.' We were in unfamiliar territory with this newly adult dynamic, and I remember the odd sidelong look my grandmother gave me when I came downstairs for dinner in a long navy-blue dress, with a classic cut that could have flattered a bus.

The day after we arrived, I very stupidly attempted to lock the front gates myself, and got in a muddle with the key in the lock. It got stuck and the latch could no longer turn properly. We stood there united in cowardice behind my grandmother's back as she rattled and fiddled with it herself, more half-heartedly than I had seen her operate before. I still feared the consequences of her wrath, and part of me opted out of mustering the energy to have a dialogue with her about the dynamics of the lock, and go through the rigmarole of fetching oil, working gloves, screwdrivers, and making a morning's crisis of it. I let her believe that it had been tampered with by somebody from outside trying to get in. She didn't seem too disturbed at this possible threat though, and it strikes me that she might have known it was me who had broken it but she too had opted out of the battle.

I knew her breaking point was not far off and we couldn't hope to spend any extra time in each other's company, so the next day, my friend and I walked all the way into the old town. As we wound along the walled road, one of the first buildings to come into view from the medieval cluster on the point was the Château Grimaldi. My friend had never seen a view like it, the ramparts overlooking pale sand where people had bathed and painted and loved long before us. When Picasso came to Antibes, France had emerged again from war; his lover Françoise was expecting his baby; they came south from Paris to the heat and light, to the territory where his friend Apollinaire had spent his childhood and to a culture closer to Picasso's native Spain than their adopted city of Paris. The blank stone spaces of the château overlooking the sharp sunlight of the Bay of Angels was the perfect setting for his studio at that moment in his life. I told my friend about how we went to see Picasso's paintings and sculptures every year, after church on Sundays or if we needed to get out of the way. But even if we did it with childish foot-dragging, lolloping behind the tourists, it was always a kind of pilgrimage we made, in homage to the master Picasso.

Picasso only stayed in Antibes for about three months in 1946, but it was an extraordinarily fertile time for him. He produced twenty-two paintings and forty-four drawings in that time. When he left, giving all of them to the Musée Grimaldi, he did so on condition that they would continue to be housed there. 'If people want to see them,' he said, 'let them come here.' They did and so did his work, over the years stacking up to three thousand pieces and only a fraction of them on display – nude women cavorting in the bright air, or voluptuous in geometric interiors decorated with star-like sea urchins and flowers. But *Two Women Running on a Beach*, the painting I knew so well from twenty summers past, was not painted in the château studio in Antibes, despite the way it seems like the quintessence of Riviera abandon. It was painted in the wake not of the Second but of the First World

War. Then, too, Picasso was expressing a new sense of fertility. He was married to his first wife, the ballerina Olga Koklova, and they had a young son. Friends had been killed in the war; others were changed or dispersed. He had acted as witness to Apollinaire at his wedding in May 1918 where, scarred and weakened from a shrapnel wound to the head, his friend married a former dancing girl who had nursed him in hospital. On their wedding night, Apollinaire and his bride dined with Picasso at the poet's flat on the Boulevard Saint-Germain. When several weeks later, Picasso too got married, Apollinaire reciprocated by being his witness. Apollinaire's marriage was the briefest. He died a few months later, his health much worsened by his head wound, by smoking and trench gas, making him prey to the flu epidemic that raged on the heels of the war.

Women Running on the Beach captures the free-flowing happiness after the war was over, but Picasso and Apollinaire knew this feeling earlier. Looking back over his life, Picasso saw those years of poverty and friendship, before fame and before the war, as his happiest. I came back to that painting of the two women, the colours so bright I could almost hold in my hand the paradox of that golden emptiness that is the air of the South. Standing in front of it now, I was half aware that my circumstances were only a temporary stopping place, the morning of something else. I hoped I could carry some of that feeling with me into the future. When we left the museum it started raining, one of the few times I've been caught in the rain in Antibes. We took shelter in a café on the old port, beneath the apartment building where Graham Greene lived and worked on most of his novels. Taking turns, we read aloud from a new English translation of Proust. It was one of those summer projects, begun in so much earnest and left unfinished at the edge of a roadside or field. It was the quiet end of the season, and as we read we gradually drew in listeners from the neighbouring tables. '*C'est magnifique,*' one of them murmured. The whole experience of that house in Antibes was becoming a tableau, a scene on which to eavesdrop, although I didn't realise that would be the last time I went there.

Dessin de Picasso

Here is the time of magic
It's coming back wait and see
A swarm of prodigies
Who haven't produced a single fable
Because we haven't imagined them yet

Depths of consciousness
We'll explore you tomorrow
And who knows what live beings
Will come from those abysses
Bringing entire universes...

Goodbye youth white Noel
When life was only a lone star
I saw its reflection
In the Mediterranean Sea
Pearlescent at a meteor

Lines from 'The Hills', first published in Apollinaire's post-war collection *Calligrammes: Poems of Peace and War 1916–1918*, and created from drafts written on active service at the front line and after he returned to Paris, wounded but alive.

ENGLAND

My father died on St Lucie's day, 13th December, 'both the year's and the day's deep midnight', John Donne's poem of the same name calls it. It is almost the darkest day of the year; for centuries it was believed to be the darkest day, a week before the modern Winter Solstice. It was 1999, and as though he could not bear to drag himself into the next millennium; as if he did not belong there, with the bright shiny aggression of the new, and the noise of the children his children gave birth to in the years following his death.

For a moment during the two days, or perhaps three or four, that my father was in hospital, I fleetingly wondered if I should bring my boyfriend with me to visit. This thought was so outrageously inappropriate I dismissed it as quickly as it arose. Once I'd articulated the idea to myself, it immediately took on a nausea-inducing repulsion. It was apparent to me that as part of the inevitable turn of events, that relationship, pleasant as it was, could not continue. I made the assumption that it was impossible to include him in what had happened, and I had a dim shade of an awareness that what had happened would continue to unfold in solitude for a long time. My father occasionally liked to mention TS Eliot's observation, more apt than most of us like to contemplate, that when the world ends it will end not with a bang, but a whimper. My own version of that was my experience, or rather, lack of experience of deathbed drama. There began and ended the fallacy of the deathbed reconciliation. How could the moment when the body gives out be the moment to dredge up for accounting, or forgiveness, or compared notes, or shared laughs, the years of misfired exchanges, ineloquent arguments and eloquent months-long gaps of nothing said?

Anyway, there were no long tortuous days of hospital visits and bedside decorum and humiliation. That terminal journey had already been absorbed into living as if the body were merely a sack for the mind, called on for regular and fierce games of tennis, but otherwise hardly communed with. There was only a brief pause before and after an operation from which he did not recover. For a moment, called out from my office where I was working in my first proper job in publishing, I thought I had stumbled into just the sort of drama my father would have excoriated for being 'slow', 'full of clichés', and having 'no jokes in it'. I might have looked aghast at his body laid low and immobile on a hospital bed. The thin coverings did not forgive the limbs and abdomen that had grown out of proportion with one another. Their messy rumples failed to disguise the fatless form, and the way they clung to his bony outline shocked me. I advanced slowly towards this frightening display of mortality, much more horrible and shocking than the repose of death. In a lapse of sentimentality, I put out my hand. Before I could reach his, he lashed mine back with an impatient swipe, the angry rebuff of one who cannot accept help as it would be an admission of vulnerability.

Looking back, it seemed a remarkable Christmas, so many people around, staying in the house and talking of his brilliance. The distortions of my memory told me it was one of the best Christmasses we ever had, with none of the tensions that usually plagued us. We were buoyed by the anecdotes, laughing at the eccentricities we shared, proud of a knowledge confirmed in the obituaries of my father that the pen was mightier even than the mortal sword. With a jolt, an insidious flick of a shutter in my brain, the reason came back, that he was dead and it was only that single loose knot that bound so many of us together. When friends reaching all the way back to his Oxford days went back to their lives, we were left in a house full of shadows. Some friends had memories of us as those three little girls in matching dresses at my parents' parties. It seemed these memories were almost more vivid to them than the present – with a kind of significance to time and the scope of their lives that was now starting to run a fine blade through my consciousness.

The juggernaut of friends, flexing the novelty of non-stop email and pushing the boundaries of new twenty-something jobs, were swapping travel plans, sleeping partners, who was going to d-j – and who had seats in whose cars. Because in spite of all, it was the Millennium and a special way of celebrating New Year's Eve was required. On the way to Scotland, a male friend prone to showing off how fast and how long he could drive, took us up the motorway to the border in one long stretch. We reached it in the middle of the night, switching between the radio, an acid trance mix, and an old tape of TS Eliot reading from his 'Four Quartets'. In some befuddled coincidence, I heard a man's voice on the radio describing the events of one fateful night in a villa on the Côte d'Azur, and repeating the words, always with their incredulous ring, '*OMAR M'A TUER.*' I could not bring myself to say that we had been there, that summer when the lady of the house down in the South was killed. Then we were back to the clipped professorial voice, 'Time present and time past / Are both perhaps present in time future.' My head pinned to the seat, an empty vortex with black tunnelling either side of it, I could not manage to yank the words from the back of my throat to say, passingly, casually, at all, that we had always had the Robert Speight record, his reading of Eliot's poems so much more suggestive than that of the man himself. I could not say how we had done things and talked about things differently, before. My senses were filtered through the knowledge of absences that were meaningless to other people. Lost, we stopped the car to look into a blacker, starrier sky than any we could see in London, and the night was silent and still.

So many of us were staying in the house over New Year, friends I'd known for several years but in a place I had never been. My internal compass almost found a steadiness in continuing to spin away from the world I could see in front of me. 'She's doing amazingly well,' somebody reported my boyfriend as saying, the thin words thinning further. 'Your father died?' the host's mother asked me around the table at lunch, one conversation drowning out another across a chaotic grouping of old friends, new romances and hangovers. 'Yes, two weeks ago.' She made a bizarre switch of subject, talking of her friend's children and their amazing careers, fixing a haunted look on me all the while. She was taken aback, as I was, to see me dry-eyed and on two legs in public. And at the same time, it was as if an unwelcome messenger had turned up to whisper in her ear, it's got her already, see, and it will get you too. Balancing that yawning fear with the banal and ongoing was a conundrum too weird to compute in the space of small talk. I almost hoped my eyes would say that wasn't the whole story, but my mind was elsewhere.

I wore one of my mother's dresses from their party days, a long green silk gown with pearls and jet beads stitched in stylised bunches of flowers across the front. Not to deviate from the assumed roles in a crisis, everything in order, important to keep the party going, went some distant tune in my head. I had the outsider boyfriend with the enormous record collection, who failed to realise when the sound he produced turned into screeching monkeys, still grinning while fondling an outsize leather headphone by his ear, and eventually saying, 'What? What?' The speakers vibrated off the table again and most people had slunk off, but I couldn't draw the curtains yet. Rude not to see the dawn in; it was the Millennium; 'we'll only live it once.' Pushing back the dawn as much as I dared it to shine on me, I stayed awake, desperate to halt the present, searching for a way to transform it, desperate to mark this time and not have to assimilate the after-math. For a moment in the middle of the night I could try to skate another plane, making out that ghosts were not stalking me. The grey light of a Scottish day not long after the Winter Solstice still came too soon.

≫

In London, my sisters and I were thrown home from the flat we shared and called back from jobs abroad, in order to be close to our mother. My grandmother was staying, forcing herself to become a guest in our house at this time of crisis in her daughter's life. She expected to be treated with the same cheery chorus of deference that she called for on normal days. I could barely open my mouth in her company for want of knowing how to link the chirruping little girl I was supposed to be with the void I was walking into. We had already failed, it was becoming clear, failed to play the game in whatever way we were supposed to. In the cruellest world we should have known that the end had been written into our time with her already, the final goodbye made redundant. She went back to France not long after the funeral, and she did not come back for the memorial service.

We crowded out St Bride's, the church off Fleet Street known as the journalists' church, where a few years before, my father and I had seen Adrian Edmondson and Rik Mayall act out a scene from *Waiting for Godot* at the memorial for an older theatre critic, Harold Hobson. The multi-tiered spire you can see from the London bridges heading to the South Bank and the *Financial Times* building gives the church its name, because its silhouette resembles a wedding cake. 'He'll be a hard act to follow for the men in your life, you girls,' said a friend in passing at the party. She was a close friend, and she meant it sympathetically. She spoke out of love for him, and as a woman who knew what it was like to suffer for love, as the man she fell in love with loved another man. It was dawning on me, from inside the mental treacle that allowed thoughts to emerge only slowly and inarticulately in my brain, that grief might condemn me to chasing an ideal. She spoke not only from loving him with profound platonic love, but also from knowing him better, I realised was more than possible, than I now ever would myself. This is one of the strange fall-outs from losing a parent young, when we were both too young. Looking around at the crowd of middle-aged men and women, I realised many of them had known my father longer than I had or ever could. They had known him when he was young, a student, a new father, a man getting breaks and recognition, a man disappointed and getting older and showing the cracks between his ideals and his own example.

I remember, despite the fog of those months, that it was my grandmother's birthday during that time. We arranged to send her a sumptuous bunch of flowers with a card. In the post afterwards, an identical note came back to each of us: 'Your name was on the flowers I received for my birthday, for which I thank you.' With this act – fathomable only in its perversity – she drew the final line in the dust between before and after. I could no more explain it than I could explain what I was experiencing, arrested aged twenty-three as I was passing the threshold into the adult world. My grandmother's gesture was impotent to me, with my feelings so divided towards her already and in the new landscape I was falling into. But to my mother it was a double blow of cruelty. It was a double loss that left her with no family in England apart from us, her three daughters, and otherwise her one brother, his wife and their children her only family on speaking terms.

When I lost my friend, I lost the habit of conferring with somebody else on a daily basis. She gave me an anchor in other people, in another way of looking at the world. Losing my father, I lost the faith that I might find that person again. I wrestled before his death and have wrestled since with the gap between a brilliance I could not live up to, and a truculence that I sometimes still shudder from, and the parallel gap between what he showed to his friends and the world and what he showed to us his children. It was confusing to be caught between these two versions of him, one fair but unconventional, enquiring, full of the greatest vivacity of mind; the other fuming, unreachable, sometimes even openly contemptuous of his family. I knew that his character was extremely gentle – women were drawn to him as much as men, and he was often drawn more to the female half of a couple, ill-attuned to boys' club camaraderie. This was who he was, partly as the consequence of a background that did not give him the sense of entitlement many of his friends at Oxford had, but in larger part due to pure force of character.

My father was a totally different being from the people I see moving through Notting Hill now. This even hit me in the face on occasion back then, if I saw him walking down the street or across the Tube platform, his eyes fixed above and beyond, part elegant stride and part fierce gambol, pushing at the pace of his thoughts, impatient to be done with the logistics of getting places, and if I called out to him, he couldn't hear and walked straight past me.

Losing my grandfather was the loss of an enigma, one that I loved with an unformed childish love, part of it excessively formal and part primitive, like the love of trees or of the sea. His hooked nose, the basket weave *casquette*, his practical respect for wine and poetry – all this melded in my mind with the qualities of a typical Frenchman, a sort of imagined caricature that I could have easy mental recourse to. After his death I found them as if brought to life again in Apollinaire, the favourite poet we had recited together. The connection was further reinforced by their physical resemblance – Apollinaire too had the Gallic nose, the mask-like posture, the small upward sloping eyebrows and the melancholy behind the eyes. My grandmother stood in the way of my being able to go back, touch the spines and leaf through the pages in my grandfather's library. But I had the Apollinaire book, and now treasured this object from my father's few possessions. I started to read the poet more and more, as a way of tapping into feelings I found hard to articulate.

For my father most of all, I mourned the losses he suffered, or I felt he had suffered, as much as I mourned my own loss of him. If he had had the appetite, if he had been able to express more simply the sensuousness of my poet, if he had had more simplicity of character, perhaps he would have saved himself from dying young. I know he had the capacity, and perhaps if he had grown up in the hot-blooded South under open blue skies he would have been more accepting of the mundane, and of the sentiments of people around him. Perhaps he would have been more confident if he had been more accepting of his own vulnerabilities, less intent on beating them into the service of his intellect. I know that I am also referring to a part of myself that longs for the largesse of the Mediterranean. In my obsession with this poet, I have been able to resolve the losses, the flaws, create the ideal, this figure who secretly harboured a painful self-awareness of his darker nature, but was desperate not to give into it.

If my grandfather had shown me a manner of living, my father had shown me a manner of thinking. If their flaws were resolved, and the perfection of each of their qualities distilled, if the two sides of a family who were openly contemptuous of the other were melded into a peaceable whole, then this was who I would find. My poet took this role, ordering the confusion of what I mourned in one place I could visit and come back to. Navigating between these ghostly ideals, my father and my grandfather and my poet, I came to realise I was trying to weave together an absolute, an ultimate way of being that existed between the two men I knew. In the scattered facts of the poet's life, as much as in his elusiveness and power to inspire me, I identified with him and made him a receptacle for the way my father had opened my eyes to the world in too short a time. In being a figure from a complete history long past, Apollinaire began to seem a more substantial figure to me than those still walking somewhere in a world that was now gone. Waking up in the morning skinned by loss – it was far harder to look that in the face.

My father had bequeathed me such an awareness of cliché, of the disciplined relationship between thinking and expression, such a high bar of approval, that it has proved difficult for me to say anything at all. So in the years after his death, I bound myself to somebody else's story, someone longer dead and buried, from another time and place, even though this time and place, I realised, kept on bending back to ones I knew. It did not seem so strange to me to be forging this intense relationship with a dead poet. I was trying to tap an unreachable well, to touch again the enigma of personality and the gap betweens the facts. I lived a double life, functioning on the exterior but connected by a fragile net to another life, haunting archives and places of the past, as much as they haunted me. What I needed to express could only emerge in the margins, straitlaced between facts that needed to be collected and then could only exist if arranged in a particular order. Even with the effort to keep them true to verification and to the forward march of unfolding past events, my sleight-of-hand was necessary to make a stranger's story into a recognisable sequence. I needed to force this retrogression into legibility, into a sequence with onward momentum, to try, fail and fail better to make the dead live.

I had been shaped to deal only in the short sentence, the single active verb, never to resort to the flabby compromise of the adverb. But how hard it is to maintain that intellectual rigour – and how essential to stave off collapse. What I was looking for was not in the nature of objective thought. Its circular two-step kept on pulling me back to the poems I had known all along, allowing me to fix myself alone in the chimerical pursuit of matching analysis to their gossamer threads. Apollinaire's poems were a way of visiting a place with a melancholy that was controlled, and could relieve me from my disjunction with the bright young twenty-something world. Following the pathways the poet had taken a century before was a way of acting out something like the exacting set of qualities I had inherited from my father. I loved this poet whose life I became obsessed by, and who seemed to have left vestiges along the way of my life. But I loved the person who had opened my eyes to an enquiry like that, and who had given me the means to make it. By turning an emotional compulsion into an intellectual pursuit, I was attempting to prove myself worthy of my father's legacy. Then I'd remember again what Apollinaire wrote about his friend Picasso, in a remark in which as always his own concerns reverberated, 'You cannot drag your father's corpse on your back for ever.'

My father filed his last piece a few days before he died. In a peculiar symmetry, it was an essay on 'the art of the obituary' – his thoughts on its history and how he had tried to develop an approach to writing a good one. It was published posthumously, maybe a day or two after the obituaries of him ran. He had anticipated the deaths of so many, writing obituaries of well-known people in well-known fields, and remarkable people in special hidden fields. He filed them away for the right night's press deadline in an irregular way, carefully considering who should be recalled in this way, preferring not to fill the pages with 'non-entities and worthies' for the sake of filling space. He had done a great range of jobs on the paper, keeping his interests alive, determined not to become stale, and realising it never worked out well if someone clung on to the same role for too long. I can hear the echo of one of his favourite dictums, 'Power corrupts and absolute power corrupts absolutely.' I wonder if he knew that it would be his last piece, and if he cared whether he saw it in print or not. The turbulent decade of the 80s, which was his heyday, had seen hubris at home and its dismantling elsewhere, another reason why home, the country he had been born into, was so different from the country he died in. I have since wondered whether my father had anticipated no death so much as his own.

It has been strange to see his by-line on the page after his death, on that piece and on other obituaries, his succinct parcelling of somebody else's achievements, with the typical footnote as to surviving spouse and children, retrieved from the archive by that person's death. Disorienting too has been coming across some of the dread words, the banished words that showed a lazy or wrong use of language. Filler words like 'of course' and 'actually', the word 'theme', that can border on the pseudo when used about a good poem, bob up in articles I've pulled up from old box files. It is difficult to articulate anything clearly. Those occasions have been a reminder too that it is all about context, and the context that makes the words work. Here is the realisation that it is impossible always to uphold the standards one most admires, and impossible for me to carry forth the standard I so admired in him. Perhaps it was more fluid than I realised, or mattered less. Then again, maybe the 68ers had a point. 'Be realistic! Demand the impossible!' Failing to demand so much would be to pull off even less. Giving it a go is better than opting out. I know my father agreed with that.

It's been much recorded that grief has a pattern to it, conformed to by most people in a remarkable levelling of some of our most isolated moments. After a time, perhaps not long after the first year, when the seasons begin to repeat themselves and their tie to that one cataclysm weakens its grip, it is as though the veil lifts. A physical feeling arrives unannounced from the far horizon, and the fog begins to dissipate, insomnia begins to loosen its hold of your tired brain. Suddenly, it is possible to communicate more directly again, to make judgments outside of that special knowledge of loss. What is so confusing about it, and makes the feeling of loss so raw and alive, is that it is constantly pressing a dialogue that cannot exist. Pushed back before it can escape from the recesses of your mind, it runs around in circles chasing its tail, gnawing at it and repeating the hurt. Its interlocutor has gone, and filling this is a hole as palpable as a wound to the body. It leaves its traces on the suddenly chapped elbows, the patchy eyebrows and peeling scalp where trauma pushes through the skin. And then recovery begins.

Winkles codfish multiple suns and urchins of the
    setting planet
From red to green all the yellow dies
Paris Vancouver Hyeres Maintenon New York and
    the Antilles
The window opens like an orange
The beautiful fruit of the light

Closing lines from Apollinaire's 'Windows', written in a flash of spontaneous optimism as he sat having a drink with two friends in the Bar Crucifix, opposite his friend the artist Robert Delaunay's flat in the rue des Grands-Augustins, Paris, in 1912.

HOME BY WAY OF FRANCE

Not long before the First World War ended, within two months of each other, the poet and the painter got married. The newly married Picasso went for a short honeymoon to stay at a villa in Biarritz belonging to one of his informal patrons. There in the summer of 1918, a few months before Apollinaire's death aged thirty-eight, Picasso decorated the walls of the blue bedroom with these lines from one of his friend's poems:

> It was a golden time we lived on the beach
> Go early one morning barefoot without your hat
> And quick as darts the toad's tongue
> Love strikes a wound at the hearts of the mad same
>   as the wise

I know that when Apollinaire wrote about that golden time as he waited for his summons to the front line, and he alluded to the 'golden secret' and his 'secret sorrow', he wove the childhood world he rarely spoke about with his delight in the friendships of his first years as a young man in Paris. Close to death – and, before the pulse and spectacle of war, weirdly close to life – he wrote some of his major poems, and some of them not his best. At times, they gesture towards a great summation, a final paradox, an abiding image. It's a slippery task, even the greatest finality tipping into the provisional and continuous.

In the people I lost, there was a cast of mind, a store of memories. I took them along with me and guarded their insubstantial presence in my fragile net. As I entered Apollinaire's world, it reflected back to me an imaginative space lit with the same kind of light as the one that had been turned off in my exterior world. My grandmother's report of my grandfather's words years before – 'The only time I ever feel at peace is when I'm at my desk' – kept coming back to me like a description of myself spoken by the wrong person. A desk piled with books gave me the kind of peace and silence I craved, the only kind I could bear. I found a richness between those silent pages that I was afraid of not finding again in life. I found a solidity in that cerebral pursuit that, for a long time, the outside world failed to contain. I made a solitary quest into a past that still existed for me, in the archives of Paris, and the streets, buildings and the Mediterranean shoreline where Apollinaire had lived and came to write about. So absorbed in this relationship, so privately committed to an impossible partnership, off stage and invisible, it was very hard to admit anyone else into my life.

The fact of my parents' marriage was absorbed into the weave of my world, without my knowing what any of those facts were, without my exploiting its capacity for mythology. It was not exemplary in the modern sense of two individuals publicly expressing their union; it was covert and shadowed by rifts. But it was the example that went before me, and on top of it I needed to build my own version. The notion of being given away was always a sticking point. Arm in arm, my father accompanying me in a conventional role: this was so far from the way we communicated. That was before scratching the surface of the exchange of goods, chattel to master, that the tradition is based on. It's not that it would have been anathema to him even though it was against common sense; he was fond of traditions that allowed people to behave well to each other, and had the lively sense of occasion that an Oxford education had given him. The 80s trend of women being offended by men opening doors for them struck him as an unnecessary militancy. He recoiled from principled dogma and the growing culture of 'offence taken'. Even being in church together might have been forgivable on the occasion of a wedding. It was just that we had long lost the habit of making any shows of affection. I had to come to marriage my own way.

The man who is now my husband and I separated for two years. We broke off our first engagement. It was too hasty and we weren't ready, but I also sensed he was trying to stop me in my habit of running away. I had decided to spend my time with the dead poet instead. He questioned whether I loved him, and was confused because he thought he knew I did. We got engaged in Bali, after climbing a volcano, setting out in the dark at three in the morning and reaching the top for sunrise. We were floating on the violet and pink clouds that sailed over its peaks, making an optical illusion in which it was impossible to tell what was sea and what was sky, and whether the island of Lombok in the distance was real or a cloudscape reflected in the water. A few days later, he went out on his scooter for the day, to get some dive training on the south of the island. When he was an hour late back, I was worried. By the time he came in, helmet under his arm, tanned from the day outside, I was a frantic mess, thinking it would be my luck for this dream of paradise to be shattered by a terrible accident. He was amazed by the strength of my reaction, but it was another six years before we got married.

Last summer, my husband and I went to Cannes for the first time together. We had to go there as it was the film festival, and for my husband this is work. In the last few days of our stay, early one morning we drove the short distance along the coast to Antibes. I knew the best beaches to go to, and we decided to see if we could find the house where I had spent twenty summers. Maybe it was because I was seven months pregnant, but I couldn't remember the name of the road that turns off the Route du Soleil and leads up to the gates. I was trying not to make a show of scanning the signs and the landmarks along the beachside road, recognising the houses by the trees and hedges and red roofs. Then I saw it and remembered in a second. We drove up to see. The gate was new and immense. A camera on a tall arm overlooked it and high fences had been added to the garden walls. I tried the intercom, but it was silent. I don't know what I would have said, but didn't have the chance anyway, so we turned back to the beach.

It was off the road that sweeps down past Eden Roc, the extravagant hotel where apparently Madonna stays. I never have, but various friends have been there on professional jollies. I knew there was a path leading down to the beach, made of shallow paved steps and strewn with the fine dry wishbone-shaped debris of pine trees. At the bottom there is the patch of stone where I watched the beating of the octopus, and smelled *crêpes* frying off a hot metal disc. But the beach I knew had been razed to rubble, the bar removed, the jetty broken. We took the adjacent path instead, to a pebble beach and high pile of rocks, where we used to take picnics at lunchtime as the private beach restaurant was too expensive a way of feeding us children. We clambered across the rocks to find a flat one to sit on, experiencing that familiar combination of discomfort on our perch and wonder at the view, the heat, the sea inviting us in if we could get past the urchins just below where the waves broke against the land. I was at just the right level of pregnancy to manage it without losing my balance altogether. I wasn't sure exactly what we were looking for, but we found nothing but ourselves and our future.

Life is held by golden arms
Find out the golden secret
All is but a rapid flame
Where blossoms the adorable rose
And rises an exquisite scent

Final lines from 'The Hills,' from Apollinaire's
Calligrammes: Poems of Peace and War.

ACKNOWLEDGEMENTS

Guillaume Apollinaire, the book I refer to in this memoir, was written and edited by Apollinaire's first biographer Pierre-Marcel Adéma and the pioneering scholar Michel Décaudin. It was published in 1971 by *La Nouvelle Revue Française* (Paris, Éditions Gallimard) on behalf of Bahnhof-Rolandseck.

My sources for the drawings in this book are the book cited above and *Picasso and Apollinaire: The Persistence of Memory* (Berkeley, Los Angeles, London, 2008) by Peter Read. Thanks to the Beckett Estate and Faber & Faber for kind permission to quote lines from Samuel Beckett's translation of Apollinaire's poem 'Zone'; to the Picasso Administration and DACS for kind permission to reproduce drawings by Pablo Picasso. Thank you also to Monsieur Gilbert Boudar and the Bibliothèque Jacques Doucet in Paris for granting me access to the Apollinaire archive, and for permission to quote 'Le Chat'. All other translations of Apollinaire's poetry are my own.

I would like to thank Professor Peter Read for his generosity in answering my occasional questions about Apollinaire; and Peter Cheek of the *Financial Times* library.

Great thanks to everybody at Short Books, and in particular Aurea Carpenter who saw something stranger beneath the surface of my biography of the poet and took it forward in a leap of faith.

For their brilliant mixture of friendship, expertise and humour, thank you Nicola Barr, Catherine Blythe, Claire Conrad, Becky Hardie, Christopher Tayler; thank you to my loving mother and sisters for being both inspirational and patient; and to my husband James for being the compass on our roundabout journey.